EMERGING **AFRICA**

EMERGING **AFRICA**

**HOW 17
COUNTRIES
ARE LEADING
THE WAY**

Steven Radelet
With an introduction by
Ellen Johnson Sirleaf

Center for Global Development

Steven Radelet was a senior fellow at the Center for Global Development from 2002 to 2010. His research and publications focused on foreign aid, economic growth, financial crises, and trade policy in developing countries, especially in sub-Saharan Africa. He served as an economic advisor to the government of Liberia from 2005 to 2009 and was a founding co-chair of the Modernizing Foreign Assistance Network. From 2000 to 2002, he was deputy assistant secretary of the U.S. Treasury for Africa, the Middle East, and Asia. He has worked in dozens of countries and has lived for extended periods in Indonesia, The Gambia, and Western Samoa.

Copyright © 2010
CENTER FOR GLOBAL DEVELOPMENT
1800 Massachusetts Avenue, NW
Washington, DC 20036
www.cgdev.org

Emerging Africa: How 17 Countries Are Leading the Way may be ordered from:
BROOKINGS INSTITUTION PRESS
c/o HFS
P.O. Box 50370
Baltimore, MD 21211-4370
Tel.: 800-537-5487
410-516-6956
Fax: 410-516-6998
Internet: www.brookings.edu

The Center for Global Development is grateful for contributions from Jennifer Ward Oppenheimer, the Bill & Melinda Gates Foundation, and the William and Flora Hewlett Foundation in support of this work.

14 13 12 11   2 3 4 5

Library of Congress Cataloging-in-Publication data

Radelet, Steven C., 1957-
  Emerging africa : how 17 countries are leading the way / Steve Radelet ; with an introduction by Ellen Johnson Sirleaf.
      p. cm.
  Includes bibliographical references and index.
  1. Africa—Economic conditions—1960- 2. Africa—Economic policy. 3. Africa—Foreign economic relations. I. Title.

  HC800.R33 2010
  330.96—dc22

                                                                         2010026016

ISBN: 978-1-933286-51-8
eISBN: 978-1-933286-52-5

For Sam

Always Remember the Boys of West Point

CONTENTS

FOREWORD

To my surprise and pleasure, I found myself in 2003 seated next to an award-winning *New York Times* journalist on a flight from Gaborone to Johannesburg. My failure to win him over on the issue we subsequently discussed has bothered me ever since. The debate centered on a simple question: Is it more important to get the good or the bad news out of Africa?

Of course, most readers will immediately perceive that this is a false dichotomy; it is pointless to say just one or the other. A more balanced answer would be that it is important to get all types of news out of Africa, not just the atrocities in Darfur—for which the journalist received a Pulitzer three years later—but also the stunning success of Botswana's unrivalled and decades-old economic growth. Both are important.

From the perspective of some Africans, however, the coverage can seem imbalanced. When it comes at all, the good news is often delivered as an afterthought or, at its worst, as a sort of half-hearted whitewash. Indeed, such attempts often only confirm Africans' suspicions that many outside the continent do not actually believe there is any good news—at least of any magnitude—coming out of sub-Saharan Africa.

Steve Radelet's authoritative book, *Emerging Africa,* puts paid to the notion that there are few large substantive positive stories to emerge out of Africa. It represents a significant scholarly blow to the picture of the so-called hopeless continent, and it achieves this by refusing to treat sub-Saharan Africa as a single entity. Hardship and strife in one country do not cancel out real, sustained gains in another hundreds of miles away. To assert otherwise is misleading and damaging.

Radelet disaggregates Africa into three groups: (1) the 17 emerging countries, (2) the oil producers, and (3) the rest. The first group represents about 300 million people, or roughly half the population of Africa. The fundamental mission of his book is to argue that, for the last 15 years, these countries have achieved steady economic growth, a deepening of democracy, stronger leadership, and falling poverty.

In chapter 2, he examines this proposition in more detail and proposes that this change is neither transitory nor superficial, but instead is the result of five fundamental changes that are elaborated upon in the subsequent chapters: (1) more democratic and accountable governments, (2) more sensible economic policies, (3) the change in the nature of the debt crisis, (4) new technologies, and (5) the emergence of a new generation of political, economic, and social leaders—the so-called cheetah generation.

The analysis is evenhanded, and Radelet is at pains not to overstate the case. He sensibly concedes that many of these countries have a litany of flaws that may render them far from perfect, both politically and economically. Their progress is also threatened by serious challenges ahead; these are explored in the final chapter and include China, climate change, diversification, the global financial crisis, and of course HIV/AIDS. South Africa's future is also disproportionately critical, and he soberly and correctly warns us that if it takes a significant turn for the worse, all bets are off.

Of course there are important steps in the areas of health, education, diversification, and governance that these emerging countries must get right in order to sustain their fragile progress. No country can simply rest on its laurels. Finally—and this is one of my favorite parts in the book—Radelet urges the international community to design trade, aid, and other instruments with a view to this progress, calling on it to "vocally stand" with the emerging countries. President Obama's visit to Ghana in July 2009 was a clear sign that others are heeding this call.

Radelet makes a critical point that non-Africans seem to overlook: it is demoralizing for the emerging countries, some of which work so hard in the face of many challenges to achieve even small and fragile gains, when they are lumped together and dismissed as part of a disastrous whole. As limited as their gains often seem, it is time to give credit where credit is due. The media should adjust their dials, Radelet convincingly argues, and stop using a 15-year-old story that paints all with the same brush.

The sensitivity of many of these perceptions, and indeed the entire book, reflect the extraordinary wealth of experience that Radelet has built up over his lifetime in government, in academia, and at the Center for Global Development as a senior fellow. The special role he has recently played as economic adviser to the government of Liberia, an emerging African success story and a powerful demonstration of the value of good leadership and sound advice, also gives him a track record to speak with authority.

This author is no mindless Afro-optimist. He offers a balanced, considered view of African development that points strongly and squarely in the direction of a turnaround in fundamental progress for roughly half the people on the continent. This book is a critical must-read for anyone interested in the issue today.

Jennifer Ward Oppenheimer
The Brenthurst Foundation

ACKNOWLEDGMENTS

This book was taking shape for a long time, and I am deeply indebted to the many people that contributed along the way. I am particularly grateful to Jennifer Ward Oppenheimer for her encouragement, patience, and generous financial support; Edward Scott Jr. for his leadership as chair of CGD; and Nancy Birdsall for her guidance, substantive input, and other support from beginning to end of this project.

The person that perhaps has contributed the most to this effort is Ellen Johnson Sirleaf. She has inspired me with her hard work, energy, and unfailing optimism for her country of Liberia. She contributed significantly to my thinking through her insights, speeches, policy choices, and vision, and I am deeply grateful to have had the opportunity to work with her over these past few years. It is through her that I have seen emerging Africa personified.

The research and publications teams at CGD, as usual, have been first-rate. Rebecca Schutte patiently and enthusiastically helped me get out of the starting blocks and provided strong research support, and then handed the baton at the midway point to Casey Dunning, who carried it over the finish line with great energy and aplomb. Rebecca, Casey, and Molly Kinder made a special contribution in helping to research and draft sections of chapters six and seven. Paolo Abarcar did yeoman's work on finding, cleaning, and organizing the data into the many charts and tables in the book, building on the earlier foundational work by Sami Bazzi. Justin Cohan-Shapiro and Robert Fuentes provided welcome assistance at some of the earliest stages of the research. When it came time to move toward publication, John Osterman did a superb job editing and transforming the text into the final product, under the steady guidance of Lawrence MacDonald. And I am ever grateful to Sheila Herrling and Ruth Levine for their humor, support, and friendship throughout this process. I deeply appreciate the generous support the William and Flora Hewlett Foundation and the Bill & Melinda Gates Foundation have brought to this book.

Several friends and colleagues read earlier versions of the manuscript and provided a wealth of insights, comments, and suggestions that strengthened the analysis and sharpened the conclusions. I am particularly indebted to the group that gave of their time to gather at CGD in January 2010 for an extensive discussion and to provide pages of written comments: Joel Barkan, Robert Bates, Nancy Birdsall, Steve Cashin, Shanta Devarajan, Carol Lancaster, Callisto Madavo, Roger Nord, Steve O'Connell, Vijaya Ramachandran, David Roodman, and Franck Wiebe. Joel Barkan, in particular, provided several rounds of very helpful comments. Robert Bates, Andy Berg, and Steve O'Connell also supplied data that helped deepen the analysis. In addition to this group, Alan Gelb, Larry Diamond, and Duncan Boughton all provided important comments.

And last, but certainly not least, I am most grateful to my family: Carrie, Meghan, and Sam. Carrie read countless versions of earlier drafts, and—as she always does—picked me up along the way with her eternal optimism, patience, and love. Without the support and understanding of all three, this project could not have been completed.

ABOUT CGD

The Center for Global Development is an independent, nonprofit policy research organization dedicated to reducing global poverty and inequality and to making globalization work for the poor. Through a combination of research and strategic outreach, the Center actively engages policymakers and the public to influence the policies of the United States, other rich countries, and such institutions as the World Bank, the IMF, and the World Trade Organization to improve the economic and social development prospects in poor countries. The Center's Board of Directors bears overall responsibility for the Center and includes distinguished leaders of nongovernmental organizations, former officials, business executives, and some of the world's leading scholars of development. The Center receives advice on its research and policy programs from the Board and from an Advisory Group that comprises respected development specialists and advocates.

The Center's president works with the Board, the Advisory Group, and the Center's senior staff in setting the research and program priorities and approves all formal publications. The Center is supported by an initial significant financial contribution from Edward W. Scott Jr. and by funding from philanthropic foundations and other organizations.

EMERGING AFRICA

Average Growth Rates per Capita, 1996–2008

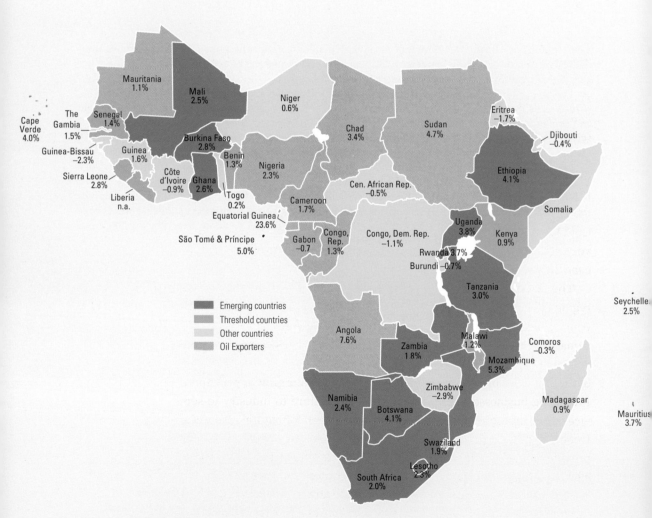

Mauritania
1.1%

Mali
2.5%

Niger
0.6%

Eritrea
−1.7%

Cape
Verde
4.0%

The
Gambia
1.5%

Senegal
1.4%

Chad
3.4%

Sudan
4.7%

Djibouti
−0.4%

Guinea-Bissau
−2.3%

Guinea
1.6%

Burkina Faso
2.8%

Benin
1.3%

Nigeria
2.3%

Ethiopia
4.1%

Sierra Leone
2.8%

Côte
d'Ivoire
−0.9%

Ghana
2.6%

Cen. African Rep.
−0.5%

Somalia

Liberia
n.a.

Togo
0.2%

Cameroon
1.7%

Equatorial Guinea
23.6%

Uganda
3.8%

Kenya
0.9%

São Tomé & Príncipe
5.0%

Gabon
−0.7

Congo,
Rep.
1.3%

Congo, Dem. Rep.
−1.1%

Rwanda 3.7%

Burundi −0.7%

Tanzania
3.0%

Seychelles
2.5%

Angola
7.6%

Zambia
1.8%

Malawi
1.2%

Mozambique
5.3%

Comoros
−0.3%

Zimbabwe
−2.9%

Madagascar
0.9%

Mauritius
3.7%

Namibia
2.4%

Botswana
4.1%

Swaziland
1.9%

Lesotho
2.3%

South Africa
2.0%

- Emerging countries
- Threshold countries
- Other countries
- Oil Exporters

INTRODUCTION

Ellen Johnson Sirleaf
President, Republic of Liberia

Twenty years ago, sub-Saharan Africa (SSA) was a region of despair. Outside of Botswana and Mauritius, democracy was but a distant dream. Unelected and unaccountable governments held power across the subcontinent. Dictators treated their countries as personal fiefdoms, taking what they wanted, doling out riches to a favored few, and sprinkling a handful of crumbs to the rest. They jailed or executed those who spoke out or whom they just didn't like, and they ruled by force and intimidation. The terrible scar of apartheid made a mockery of justice and plunged the entire southern region into conflict and crisis. And the politics of the Cold War made a bad situation worse, as East and West propped up unsavory rulers for their own purposes with little regard for the effect on Africans themselves.

The leadership crisis translated into an economic crisis that left the region effectively bankrupt. Authoritarian leaders used the state to try to control the economic commanding heights, in part to finance their patronage systems. In the end, their control only destroyed economic assets and personal livelihoods. For 20 years starting in the mid-1970s, nearly all of the countries of SSA saw zero or negative economic growth per capita. Promising businesses were ruined, from agriculture to industry to services. New investment stopped, except for the grab for natural resources. Unemployment soared, and working men and women could no longer provide for their families. Schools and health facilities deteriorated badly. The only things that seemed to thrive were poverty and conflict.

My own country of Liberia tells the terrible tale. Riven by a tragic history of ethnic conflict, exclusionary politics, and authoritarian rule, Liberia plunged into violence in the 1980s and was nearly destroyed by a senseless civil war. An estimated 270,000 people were killed—about 1 in 12 Liberians—and hundreds of thousands more fled their homes. Families were uprooted, communities were destroyed, and infrastructure was left in ruins. Children spent more time at war than at school. The warlords used violence and intimidation to loot our national assets, smuggle diamonds, and traffic in arms and drugs. Anguish and misery were everywhere.

But that was then. Today, all of that has begun to change. The era of the warlords is over and has been replaced by a new era of democratic governance. Since the war ended in 2003, Liberians have not only maintained the peace, they have seized the opportunity to begin to build the foundations for democracy, economic recovery, and lasting prosperity. In 2006, I became Africa's first elected woman president. That moment was seen around the world as one of hope and possibility, not just for Liberia, but for the region more broadly. Our people, in a free and fair election, gave my government the greatest opportunity that can come to any leader—the chance to rebuild a nation from the ruins of war.

Our objectives are both simple and ambitious. Liberians want to build a new nation that is peaceful, secure, and prosperous, with democratic and accountable governance based on the rule of law, and with abundant employment and other economic opportunities. We know it will be a long process. While everyone is impatient for change, myself included, we know that it will take time to undo the damage done by generations of misrule and to establish a strong foundation for the future. But we are on our way.

In just the last four years, we have rehabilitated hundreds of schools. We have more than doubled primary school enrollment, literally putting thousands of children back in school, with a special focus on young girls. We have more than doubled the number of health facilities that are providing a basic package of health services, and have increased immunization rates for yellow fever and polio to above 90 percent. We are beginning to see declines in the prevalence of malaria, cholera, and anemia.

We have established an anticorruption commission and revitalized the General Auditing Commission. We have increased the transparency of our public finances, and we are proud that in 2009 Liberia became the first country in all of Africa to become fully compliant with the Extractive Industries Transparency Initiative (EITI), a global standard for revenue transparency in oil, gas, and minerals. Whereas we had inherited nearly US$5 billion in overdue and unpayable debts from previous administrations, we worked with the international community so that by mid-2010 we had eliminated almost all of it through the Heavily Indebted Poor Country (HIPC) Initiative.

We are rebuilding roads and bridges across the country and have brought light and water back to the capital city for the first time in 14

years. In 2009, we ranked among the top 10 most improved in the world in the World Bank's Doing Business Survey. These steps are paying off: we have more than doubled total investment and more than tripled government revenues. Our economy has grown by a robust 7 percent per year for the past five years, and average incomes have increased by 20 percent.

Across at least half of sub-Saharan Africa, similar changes are under way. What is happening in Liberia is but a microcosm of the transformations that are sweeping across many African countries. Dictators are being replaced by democracy. Authoritarianism is giving way to accountability. Economic stagnation is turning to resurgence. And most important, despair is being replaced by hope—hope that people can live in peace with their neighbors, that parents can provide for their families, that children can go to school and receive decent health care, and that people can speak their minds without fear.

In this important book, Steve Radelet describes and analyzes the deep changes taking place across emerging Africa. It is a breath of fresh air in that it does not treat SSA as a monolithic entity, but instead recognizes that countries across the region have distinctive histories, endowments, and political systems, and that they are on different trajectories going forward. It puts aside both the typical pessimistic view that the entire subcontinent is in continual crisis and the overly optimistic view that the entire region has undergone transformation. It carefully dis-

sects and explores the divergent trends under way. It focuses in on a group of 17 emerging countries that have undergone dramatic economic and political changes since 1995, along with six other countries where there has been positive but less dramatic change, or—like Liberia—where these transformational changes have been under way for a shorter period of time.

The changes in the emerging countries since the mid-1990s are striking. Investment is growing quickly. Foreign investors that never would have thought of Africa a decade ago are lining up to look at new opportunities. Trade is expanding even more rapidly as businesses become more integrated with global markets. GDP is growing by more than 5 percent per year, so that average incomes in the emerging countries have increased by 50 percent since the mid-1990s. Political conflict has subsided, and governments are strengthening the protection of civil liberties and political freedoms. Most of the emerging countries have embraced democracy, and their ratings on a range of governance indicators are improving. More youth are in school, from primary schools through universities, and health care has improved significantly. Poverty rates have been falling by one full percentage point per year for more than a decade, ushering in the most rapid decline in poverty rates ever seen on the continent. The differences between the despair and misery of the 1980s and the hope and energy of today are like night and day.

Radelet describes five fundamental changes that have fueled this transformation and set the foundation for continued resurgence in the years ahead, including the rise of democracy and more accountable governments, the introduction of stronger economic policies, the end of the long debt crisis and concurrent strengthening of relationships with the international community, the introduction of cell phones and other new technologies, and the emergence of a new generation of private and public leaders. His analysis shows the importance of each of these key changes, both individually and in concert, complementing and strengthening each other.

For me the most important is the change in political systems, leadership, and governance. I've often said that Liberia is not a poor country, but rather a rich country that has been poorly managed. The same is true for most of SSA. Africa's crisis was a failure of leadership and management. Sub-Saharan Africa is rich in resources, talent, energy, and spirit. But it has not been rich in leadership. It is made up of rich countries that were poorly managed, and the results have been disastrous.

Good leadership is only partly about the individual people in the leadership positions. Much more important is how these leaders are chosen and how they are held accountable by their citizens. Africa has had many well-educated presidents and prime ministers who initially looked as if they might be good leaders, but they failed because they had too much centralized power and because basic systems of checks and balances and accountability did not function. Finding good leaders and sustaining good leadership requires establishing freedom of speech, freedom of political discourse, free and fair elections, transparency of government actions, and checks and balances through strong legislatures and judicial systems. As the emerging countries of Africa continue to build these institutions of accountability, I am confident that skillful leaders will emerge and that they will be able to lead effectively.

For more than a century, Africa's fate was more often than not decided by people beyond its shores. But not anymore. The future of the emerging countries is in the hands of their own people. It is Africans who must determine their own economic policies, make choices about how to manage their budgets and spend scarce resources, decide how to encourage new technologies and expand trade throughout the region and with the rest of the world, make choices about the highest priorities in their development strategies, and establish their own strong systems for accountable governance. The record in the emerging countries on these issues since the mid-1990s has been strong, and there are good reasons to be optimistic that they can continue their success into the future.

At the same time, the international community has an essential supporting role to play. One important means of support is foreign assistance. Aid is clearly not the most important factor in Africa's development, nor is it always as effective as it could be. But those who argue that aid has failed, or that aid was somehow the cause of SSA's collapse, have it wrong. Their arguments are at least a decade out of date. They fail to see the transformational changes that are under way and the supporting role that foreign assistance has played. In Liberia, the backing of the international community has been crucial in supporting the work of the United Nations Mission in Liberia (UNMIL); helping to rebuild roads, schools, and clinics; and providing valuable advice on a range of important issues. Donor support and good governance have triggered billions of dollars in new private investment; together, they have laid the foundation for Liberia to continue to move forward. Without this international support, Liberia would not have made nearly as much progress and might have even plunged back into conflict. Across the emerging countries, as donors have moved to more country-led approaches for development and poverty reduction, aid has been increasingly effective in making important contributions to the economic turnaround. That said, much can be done to make aid even more effective. Donors should simplify bureaucratic procedures, align assistance more closely to government priorities, speed the delivery process, and focus more on building capacity and strengthening local systems that can be sustained over time.

It's not just aid and investment; the emerging countries need to expand trade. The industrialized countries must open their borders to much greater trade from low-income countries. If for political reasons they cannot reduce trade barriers to all developing countries, they should focus first on the countries that are taking major steps to improve governance and escape poverty—such as the emerging countries—that have a chance to stimulate new exports, increase their self-reliance, and over time reduce their reliance on aid. If the emerging countries are to sustain their success, they must be able to stand on their own feet and sell products around the world on open markets. Trade barriers in the rich countries make our very difficult job even more challenging. All we ask for is a level playing field.

It is an exciting and encouraging time for Africa's emerging countries. We have put behind us the conflict and misery of the past and replaced them with peace and opportunity. We know that the challenges are great, and our success is far from assured. But our hopes are growing and our confidence is expanding as we continue to deepen our economic recovery, build stronger democracies, fight poverty, and build a brighter future for our people. I urge you to read on to learn more about the exciting transformations under way in emerging Africa.

EMERGING **AFRICA**

There's good news out of Africa. Not all of Africa. But from a large part of Africa that quietly, with little fanfare, is on the move.

Seventeen emerging African countries are putting behind them the conflict, stagnation, and dictatorships of the past. Since the mid-1990s—*for fifteen years*—they have achieved steady economic growth, deepening democracy, stronger leadership, and falling poverty. Six additional African countries are showing signs of following their lead. The old negative stereotypes of sub-Saharan Africa don't apply to these countries. Not anymore.

Consider Ghana, where over the past 15 years the economy has grown by a robust 5 percent per year, translating into annual growth in income per person of 2.6 percent per year, well above the global average of 1.9 percent. As a result, the income of the average Ghanaian has increased by more than 40 percent. Investment has doubled, and so have exports. Primary school enrollment has increased by one-third, life expectancy has reached 60 years, and the population growth rate has dropped from 3.5 percent to 2 percent. The share of the population living below the poverty line has plummeted from 50 percent to less than 30 percent.[1] And Ghana has become a vibrant democracy, with competitive elections, a vocal press, better protection of basic rights, and stronger governance. Ghana is far from perfect, but it is much stronger politically, economically, and institutionally than it was just 15 years ago.

---

1 Poverty rates, based on a poverty line of US$1.25 in purchasing power per day (US$450 per year), are drawn from the World Bank's PovcalNet database online. See also Shaohua Chen and Martin Ravallion, "The Developing World Is Poorer Than We Thought, But No Less Successful in the Fight against Poverty," World Bank Policy Research Working Paper no. 4703 (August 2008), http://go.worldbank.org/KMTYCLRA30 . Unless otherwise stated, all other data are drawn from the World Bank's World Development Indicators online.

Or Mozambique, where GDP has grown a remarkable 7.5 percent per year for 15 years, one of the fastest growth rates in the world. Average real income has more than doubled. Primary school enrollment has jumped from 42 percent to over 70 percent, the debt-to-GDP ratio has dropped from 330 percent to 40 percent, and poverty has fallen from 84 percent to 64 percent. Financial returns on investment have increased sharply, and foreign investment has jumped from 1 percent to 5 percent of a much larger GDP. Multiple peaceful elections have gone hand in hand with improvements in a wide range of governance and democracy indicators.

Then there is Mali, which despite being a landlocked desert country has quietly achieved GDP growth of 5.5 percent per year since the mid-1990s. Infant mortality is down 25 percent, the primary school completion rate has doubled, and poverty has fallen by about one-third. Mali, too, has established a thriving multiparty democracy with competitive elections, a free press, better protection of civil liberties and political rights, less corruption, and stronger governance.

In Tanzania, economic growth has averaged a robust 5.7 percent since the mid-1990s, leading to an increase in average incomes of 46 percent since 1996. Exports were just 11 percent of GDP in 1991; today they are more than 20 percent of a larger GDP. Meanwhile, external debt has been cut from 160 percent of GDP to just 30 percent. Infant mortality has declined by 25 percent, and the population growth rate has dropped from 3.3 percent to 2.4 percent. Tanzania, like the other countries, has shifted toward democratic governance, with multiple peaceful elections, stronger adherence to political and civil rights, and stronger governance.

In Cape Verde, GDP has grown 6 percent per year since 1993, leading to a welcome 66 percent increase in average income. Exports have doubled from 10 percent to 20 percent of GDP. In 1990, just 54 percent of children completed primary school; today it is nearly 90 percent. Infant mortality rates have been nearly cut in half, from 45 to 24 per 1,000 since 1990. Poverty rates have halved from 40 percent to less than 20 percent in just 15 years. Multiple peaceful and fair elections have transformed the country into a thriving democracy.

The really good news is that Ghana, Mozambique, Mali, Tanzania, and Cape Verde are not alone. They are part of a growing and dynamic group of emerging African countries that are breaking away from the dismal histories of economic decline and political decay commonly associated with Africa. They are defying the usual pessimistic African storylines of war, famine, stagnant economies, deepening poverty, destructive political leadership, and poor governance. Largely unnoticed by the outside world, these countries are quietly setting themselves apart from the old norms, with more accountable and democratic governments, rising incomes, new investment opportunities, less corruption, improved health and education, and declining poverty.

It is time to think anew about Africa. Or to be more precise, it's time to think anew about Africa's emerging countries.

✳ ✳ ✳

For more than 30 years, it has seemed that just about all of the news out of Africa has been bad. Newspapers report endless civil wars, repeated coups, gross misrule, famine, disease, and poverty across the continent. Academics, pundits, and Western politicians decry the failures and misdeeds of private investors, foreign aid agencies, or African leaders and paint a picture of a continent in perpetual crisis.

There surely has been much failure, conflict, and stagnation. And deep challenges continue in places like the Democratic Republic of the Congo (DRC), Somalia, Sudan, and Zimbabwe.

But the image of an entire continent mired in failure and hopelessness is increasingly out of date. As important as are the tragedies in DRC, Sudan, Somalia, and Zimbabwe, and as deserving as they are of urgent international attention, too often they are seen to typify the continent as a whole. But nothing could be further from the truth.

For too long, politicians, the media, academic researchers, and casual commentators have blended together all the countries of sub-Saharan Africa (SSA), treating the countries of the region as a single entity, and sometimes even as a single country. But this aggregate continent-wide approach is overdone. It completely misses, or misreads, important events and changes. It combines improvements in one country with deterioration in another, and concludes that nothing is changing when quite the opposite is true. It generates sweeping generalizations about the continent that at best apply to some countries, but far from all. It misleads the world about Africa.

Sub-Saharan Africa is a region rich in diversity with significant differences in history, economic potential, geography, culture, and political systems.[2] While the countries across the region share some common characteristics, one of the clearest patterns since the mid-1990s has been significant *divergence* in economic performance and political change.

These differences make it increasingly difficult to look at SSA as a single entity with common patterns, or to make sweeping diagnoses and recommendations about the subcontinent as a whole. The abysmal political and economic situation in Zimbabwe has little in common with the dynamism of Ghana. The challenges facing Somalia are completely different

---

2 For an excellent and very readable overview of the main issues, trends, and players in Africa's contemporary development, see Todd Moss, *African Development: Making Sense of the Issues and Actors* (Boulder, CO: Lynne Rienner Publishers, 2007).

from those facing Mali. And the major issues confronting the DRC bear little resemblance to those of vibrant Mozambique. This is not to say that what happens in one country does not affect others in the region, or that there are not common issues that affect all countries across the region. But it is to say that broad analyses and simple generalizations make little sense when economic performance and political systems have diverged so much in the last 15 years.

The world has understood this about Asia for some time. When analysts discuss the spectacular economic performance in "Asia" during the last 40 years, they do not mean Asia as a whole. They do not lump together North Korea with South Korea, Myanmar with Thailand, Papua New Guinea with Indonesia, or Laos with China. They have long understood that while some countries in the region share important trends and achievements, not all countries do, and that it makes little sense to put them all together in one analytic pot of stew. They know that the remarkable democratic progress in Indonesia during the last 10 years is not made suspect by its absence in Cambodia, and that the economic dynamism of Malaysia is not somehow cheapened by the stagnation in Nepal. It is time to begin to make similar distinctions in Africa.

The Emerging Countries of Africa

This book—which builds on an earlier paper coauthored with President Ellen Johnson Sirleaf of Liberia[3]—is about a group of 17 emerging African countries comprising more than 300 million people that since the mid-1990s have begun to undergo dramatic changes in economic growth, poverty reduction, and political accountability. Another six countries have seen promising but less dramatic or less sustained change, a group I refer to as the threshold countries. Together these 23 countries account for nearly half of SSA's 48 countries.

These countries, listed in Table 1.1, are spread across western, eastern, central, and southern Africa. Most are coastal, but several are landlocked. Their colonial histories differ widely. Importantly, none of them are oil exporters. I purposely exclude oil exporters from the group even though several have grown rapidly in recent years because the underlying dynamics in oil-exporting countries are very different and the foundations for sustained progress are far more open to question. The emerging countries are not defined by commodity booms. While prices for many exports have

---

3 Ellen Johnson Sirleaf and Steven Radelet, "The Good News out of Africa: Democracy, Stability, and the Renewal of Growth and Development," Center for Global Development Essay (2008), http://www. cgdev.org/content/publications/detail/15416/.

TABLE 1.1 Income Growth in the Emerging African Countries

	Annual Income Growth per Capita 1996–2008		Cumulative Increase in Average Real Income, 1996–2008
Emerging Countries			
Botswana	4.1%		68%
Burkina Faso	2.8%		43%
Cape Verde	4.0%		67%
Ethiopia	4.1%		65%
Ghana	2.6%		40%
Lesotho	2.3%		33%
Mali	2.5%		37%
Mauritius	3.7%		61%
Mozambique	5.3%		96%
Namibia	2.4%		36%
Rwanda	3.7%		60%
São Tomé and Príncipe	5.0%		40%
Seychelles	2.5%		37%
South Africa	2.0%		29%
Tanzania	3.0%		46%
Uganda	3.8%		61%
Zambia	1.8%*		25%
Average	**3.2%**		**50%**
Threshold Countries			
Benin	1.3%		18%
Liberia	3.1%	2005–2008	13%
Kenya	2.4%	2003–2008	15%
Malawi	1.2%		15%
Senegal	1.4%		20%
Sierra Leone	3.7%	2003–2008	24%

* Zambia is included even though its 13-year growth rate is slightly lower than 2 percent because its annual average growth rate for the 10-year period 1999–2008 was 2.3 percent.

Source: World Bank, World Development Indicators; data for South Africa are from the South African Reserve Bank.

risen rapidly in recent years, on the whole commodity prices have moved *against* these countries since the mid-1990s. Some of the emerging countries are small, but with 300 million people, collectively they are not small; they are roughly equivalent to France, Germany, Italy, Spain, and the United Kingdom combined. Together they number about 1 out of 20 people in the world.

What they share is a clear break from the past and the beginnings of a wide-ranging economic, political, and development turnaround dating back to the mid-1990s. Consider some of the key changes in these countries, which are described in more detail in chapter 2:

- Economic growth rates in each country have been *at least* 2 percent per capita since 1996, and have averaged 3.2 percent per capita, equivalent to overall GDP growth of *more than 5 percent per year.*

- The share of people living below the poverty line (income of US$1.25/day) dropped from 59 percent in 1993 to 48 percent by 2005—a huge drop for a 12-year period.

- Trade and investment have more than doubled, and financial returns on investment are much higher.

- School enrollment, school completion, and literacy rates are all increasing. Education levels for girls, in particular, are rising from their once abysmally low levels.

- Health indicators are generally improving, with the exceptions of countries badly affected by the HIV/AIDS pandemic. For example, child mortality (deaths under five years old) averaged 134 per 1,000 in 1985 in these 17 countries; today it averages less than 102, meaning that 32 more children out of every 1,000 are living to see their fifth birthday.

- Both population growth and fertility rates have begun to decline.

Consider the economic turnaround in the emerging countries: for two decades between 1975 and 1995, they recorded economic growth per capita of essentially zero. But between 1996 and 2008, they achieved growth per capita averaging 3.2 percent per year, powering a full 50 percent increase in average incomes in just 13 years. Think of that change for a moment: from 20 years of no growth in income to 13 years during which average incomes increased by half. This is a huge turnaround. Something has changed.

Critically, there are equally significant changes in political systems and governance. Across Africa, democracies are replacing dictatorships. The era of the prototypical African "big man" is not quite over, but it is drawing to a close. According to widely used international indicators of political rights, civil liberties, and political institutions, the number of countries meeting basic standards of democracy in Africa has grown from just 3 in 1989 to more than 20 today, including 13 of the 17 emerging countries. And this is *not* just about holding elections; the changes are deeper, with greater adherence to basic standards of political rights and civil liberties, more freedom of the press, a much more vibrant civil society, greater transparency, and stronger checks and balances. And there has been marked improvement in the quality of governance as measured by several different independent indicators, reflecting less conflict and political violence, stronger adherence to the rule of law, and lower levels of corruption.

To be sure, these countries are far from perfect. They face many tough challenges, and their continued success is far from certain. It is not as if they can just sit back and relax and assume that compound economic growth will work its magic and automatically propel them to prosperity. The political and economic turnaround remains fragile. Although poverty rates are falling, large numbers of people continue to live in dire poverty. Education and health systems, while clearly improving, remain substandard. The business environment is better, but remains weak. Corruption is lower and the rule of law stronger, but there is a long way to go. And the movement toward democracy and better governance has had many shortcomings, some reversals, and very uneven progress. It clearly has not gone far enough.

But the transformation since the mid-1990s is clear. Something deep is at work. These countries are on a different path from the one they were on in the past, and on a much different path from the one other countries in the region have followed.

Five Fundamental Changes

What ignited the turnaround in the emerging countries? Can the promising trends over the last 15 years be continued? Is the revival simply the result of changes in commodity prices or the business cycle that are likely to be reversed? Or is it the beginning of a new era for these countries? The turnaround is neither cyclical nor temporary. It is not just a blip on the screen, nor just a result of commodity prices. The revival is now 15 years in the making. It persisted through a global recession and falling commodity prices in the late 1990s. It has continued even though import prices have risen faster than export prices for these countries. And these countries appear to have weathered the 2009 global economic crisis better than most developing countries. All of these facts —and more—suggest that much more than the business cycle is at work.

Rather, this book shows that the turnaround reflects much more fundamental changes taking place in the political, economic, and social spheres of these countries. These changes are the beginnings of a transformation—fraught with risks and with no guarantee of ultimate success—that provides a stronger foundation for continued economic growth, political evolution, and poverty reduction in the future.

At least five fundamental changes are at work. The first two—the rise of more democratic and accountable governments and the introduction of more sensible economic policies—together ignited the turnaround in the 1990s and have helped sustain it over time. The next three—the end of the debt crisis and changing relationships with the international community, the spread of new technologies, and the emergence of a new generation of public and private leaders—began to kick in after the recovery had begun, but they have been critical to continuing it over time. Looking forward, it is the *combination of all five* that provides the promise that emerging Africa's initial success can be sustained and expanded into the future. Let's take a brief look at these five key changes.

1. **The rise of more democratic and accountable governments.** Africa's growth and development tragedy has been, in large part, a failure of leadership. Too many African leaders have ruled by intimidation, violence, and brute force. But in the 1980s, as the economic crisis deepened, many authoritarian governments lost both the last shards of their legitimacy and the economic and financial resources they needed to maintain control. Protestors began to call for economic and political change, and governments lost the backing of key supporters. With the end of the Cold War and apartheid in the early 1990s, authoritarian leaders increasingly were forced to give way to democratically elected governments. The number of democracies in SSA jumped from just 3 in 1989 to 23 in 2008, including most of the emerging countries.

   Crucially, democracy has not just meant elections but greater adherence to basic political and civil rights, more freedom of the press, and stronger political institutions. And in the emerging countries, the shift toward democracy has gone hand in hand with improvements in the quality of governance more broadly. The movement toward democracy and better governance has been uneven and remains incomplete. But it is real. It has been at the core of the renaissance in these countries, and it is fundamental to continued progress in the future.

2. **The implementation of more sensible economic policies.** Twenty years ago, nearly all African economies were effectively bankrupt, with large budget deficits, double-digit inflation, growing debt burdens, thriving black markets, shortages of basic commodities, and rising poverty. Economic mismanagement and the heavy hand of the state scared off investors, generated capital flight, and led to stagnation and rising poverty.

   But in the late 1980s, economic policies began to change in the emerging countries, and they have continued to gradually change over time. Today they bear little resemblance to the past. Black markets are but a distant memory. Budget and trade deficits are more sustainable. The business environment is friendlier, and trade and investment barriers have been reduced. Marketing boards have largely disappeared, and there is a better balance between the state and the private sector. As with governance, the changes in economic policy are far from perfect, but they are vastly improved from 20 years ago and are central to sustaining growth and development in the future.

It was the interplay between economic reform and political change that ignited the turnaround. The economic crisis itself contained the seeds of political change. As the crisis deepened in the 1980s, the failures of past approaches became starkly evident, and borrowing and other financing options disappeared. The old approaches could no longer be financed. Governments were forced to adopt economic reforms and austerity measures to close their budget and trade deficits. The austerity measures accelerated protests and calls for change. Whereas in the past, authoritarian governments had been able to minimize the impact of protests by using budget resources and other measures to placate civil servants, favored businesses, the military, and other supporters, by the late 1980s many no longer had the financial or political resources to do so. The winds of global change gave the final push: as the Cold War and apartheid ended, strong forms of socialism and authoritarian control fell into disrepute. People across Africa were fed up with the old systems. Forced to hold elections, most governments were replaced by more pluralistic and democratic regimes.

The economic policy reforms initially had little effect on economic growth, in large part because political instability grew sharply in the early 1990s with the uncertainty around the new elections. But as the political changes began to stabilize—especially following the election of Nelson Mandela as the president of South Africa in 1994—confidence began to grow and economies began to respond. The revitalization of emerging Africa had begun.

A succinct version of the key changes in the early 1990s in the emerging countries is shown in Figure 1.1. The top panel shows the broad pattern of changes in economic policy, encapsulated by changes in the prevalence of so-called antigrowth syndromes, a term coined by the landmark *Economic Growth in Africa* research project undertaken by the African Economic Research Consortium (heretofore the AERC growth project).[4] The research team identified four syndromes that were at the core of Africa's poor economic performance (described in more detail in chapter 4). Three were directly related to economic policy: heavy-handed control regimes, redistribution systems that rewarded political allies and ethnic groups at the expense of economic growth, and heavy borrowing and asset stripping that sacrificed future income for present gain. (The fourth syndrome was state breakdown and political instability.) Notice the sharp reduction in syndromes in the emerging countries beginning in the mid-1980s—a clear indication

---

4 Benno Ndulu, et al., *The Political Economy of Economic Growth in Africa, 1960–2000,* vols. 1 and 2 (Cambridge: Cambridge University Press, 2007).

of the introduction of strong economic policy reforms. Remarkably, by 1995 the emerging countries were essentially syndrome-free.

The middle chart depicts the changes in political systems in the emerging countries, as captured by the improvements in Freedom House's indices of political rights and civil liberties. Political change began in force in 1989 and 1990, slightly after the initiation of economic changes, and accelerated rapidly throughout the early 1990s.

The bottom panel shows the economic renaissance in the emerging countries, as indicated by the rapid increase in income per capita. As the antigrowth syndromes were removed and the political changes stabilized in the mid-1990s, economic growth began to accelerate, and corresponding improvements in a wide variety of other economic, social, and poverty indicators came in to play. By 2008, incomes per capita had increased by an average of 50 percent.

This chart hints at one of the core messages of this book: the strong and positive relationship between democratic governance and economic performance in Africa. Globally, there has been an animated debate about whether authoritarian or democratic governments have been associated with stronger economic performance in developing countries over the last several decades.[5] The overall relationship is mixed, but in Africa the relationship is crystal clear: democratic governments (starting with Botswana and Mauritius in the 1970s) have been successful, while authoritarian governments have by and large been failures.

3. **The end of the decades-long debt crisis, and with it major changes in Africa's relationship with the international community.** The 1980s debt crisis hit Africa particularly hard. Stagnant economies and heavy borrowing—a result of both poor economic management by the borrowers and aggressive lending by some of the creditors—created huge debt burdens by the late 1980s that weighed down these economies and made the challenge of recovery even greater. As the crisis deepened, the International Monetary Fund (IMF) took on a much more prominent role in Africa, and IMF–World Bank "stabilization and structural adjustment" programs became the centerpiece of both economic policymaking and the relationship between African countries and the donor community.

Today, nearly 25 years after its onset, the debt crisis is finally winding down for most African countries. Debt burdens are significantly

---

5 For a recent contribution that provides strong evidence in favor of democracies over nondemocracies, see Morton Halperin, Joseph Siegle, and Michal Weinstein, *The Democracy Advantage: How Democracies Promote Prosperity and Peace* (New York: Routledge, 2010).

FIGURE 1.1 Major Changes in the Emerging Countries: Economic Policy Reform, Political Change, and Income per Capita

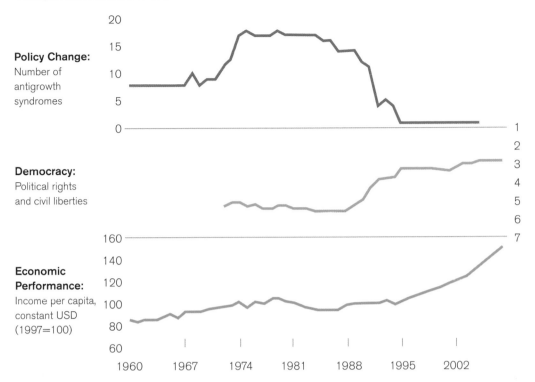

Sources: Antigrowth syndromes are from the AERC Africa growth project, political rights and civil liberties are from Freedom House, and income per capita is from the World Bank's World Development Indicators.

lower than they were just 10 years ago, freeing up financial resources and relieving the time burden on senior policymakers who no longer need to constantly reschedule huge debts.

But just as important, as debt burdens have fallen, relationships between these countries and the donor community have fundamentally changed. Country-led poverty reduction strategies have replaced the heavy conditionality of IMF and World Bank stabilization and structural adjustment programs as the centerpiece of economic policymaking and of donor programs. The IMF's role is less dominant than it once was, and donor conditions are, imperfectly, more in line with country priorities. As debt burdens have fallen and economic policies have improved, relationships with donors have become much healthier and less adversarial, providing a stronger basis for donor support to bolster future development in the emerging countries.

4. **The spread of new technologies that are creating new opportunities for business and political accountability.** Cell phones are becoming ubiquitous across Africa, and internet access is growing quickly. It seems as though there is a cell phone in every hand and an internet café on every street corner, and they have an enormously wide range of applications. In the most remote corners of the countryside, they are being used to relay information on prices and shipments in real time and to facilitate the transfer of funds and banking services with simple text messages. Cell phones are enabling health-care workers to provide early warnings of disease outbreaks and transmit and maintain reliable health information for better case management. At the same time, the internet is shrinking distances, facilitating the flow of information, and helping overcome geographical boundaries. Although so far the internet has had less impact than cell phones, it is opening up new economic opportunities and creating jobs that did not exist before, such as data entry and other services. And both are widening political involvement by enabling the debate and the flow of information that are the backbone of political accountability and transparency.

These new technologies are raising economic productivity, increasing incomes, helping to deliver basic services, and facilitating transparency and accountability, all of which strengthen the prospects for continued growth and development in these countries. And their influence will only grow in the years to come.

5. **The emergence of a new generation of policymakers, activists, and business leaders.** A new generation of political, social, and economic leaders is emerging across Africa. They are Africans to the core, but with a globalized outlook that comes through the age of the internet and easy air travel that has allowed many to live and attend school abroad and exposed them to international ideas. They are savvy, sharp, and entrepreneurial, capable of combining the best of both worlds. They can be found rising through the ranks of government, starting up businesses, working as local representatives of multinational corporations, leading local NGOs and activist groups, and taking an increasing role in political leadership. They are fed up with the unaccountable governments and economic stagnation of the past and are bringing new ideas and new vision.

Africa's future lies with them, and at the moment that future looks increasingly bright.

Collectively, these five changes provide the promise for the future. They provide the cornerstones for the emerging countries to sustain and build on their initial success, further deepen democracy, strengthen account-ability and good governance, create more—and more broad-based—economic opportunities, fight disease and illiteracy, and reduce poverty.

Readers who have been around Africa for a long time are saying right about now: Wait a minute . . . haven't we been here before? Didn't many countries in Africa record rapid growth in the 1960s only to see it all col-lapse? Yes they did. Côte d'Ivoire, Kenya, and several other countries ex-perienced robust economic growth for over a decade. SSA as a whole gen-erated growth per capita of just over 1 percent per year between 1960 and 1977. But today's emerging countries differ in several key ways. They are more numerous, they are growing faster, and they already have been growing longer than those of the earlier period. Moreover, they have a stronger foundation on which to sustain their progress, starting with more accountable and democratic governance. Their politics and eco-nomics are not caught in the great schism of the Cold War or weighted down by the primacy of the break from colonialism. Instead, their eco-nomic policies are much closer to the kinds of approaches that have been successful in other developing countries. And perhaps most important, there is a new generation of government and business leaders who have learned from the mistakes of the past and are determined not to repeat them. The experience of the 1960s should temper our optimism, but should not nullify it. Something deeper is going on in these countries.

Breaking Out of Traps?

One way to think about the emerging countries is through the lens of de-velopment traps. The notion of a "poverty trap" in which low income traps individuals and countries in perpetual poverty is an old idea and has some appeal. After all, as the saying goes, the rich get richer and the poor get left behind. Or, if you like, it takes money to make money. But as a gen-eral proposition, a pure poverty trap focused on income alone doesn't hold up very well. If it were true, since the whole world was poor 300 years ago, we would all still be poor, and countries like China and Indone-sia could not have made the phenomenal progress that they have made in recent years. Instead, most of the world is much better off than it was even 50 or 100 years ago.[6]

But in recent years the idea of traps has been advanced and refined by economists Jeffrey Sachs, Paul Collier, and others who go beyond a pure

---

6 Paul Collier makes this same point in *The Bottom Billion: Why the Poorest Countries Are Failing and What Can Be Done About It* (New York: Oxford University Press, 2007), 5.

poverty trap and suggest that certain low-income countries face particular constraints and circumstances other than just low incomes that make it much more difficult to fight poverty. Sachs's work has emphasized health and geography traps.[7] Endemic disease, such as malaria and AIDS, reduces worker productivity and scares away investors, keeping people poor and even more vulnerable to disease. And since people are poor, the potential vaccine market is not substantial enough for pharmaceutical companies to invest significantly in new products. So countries with endemic disease can get stuck in poverty. Breaking away is not impossible, but it is not easy. Similarly, adverse geography, such as inaccessible terrain or poor climate, also preserves poverty. Poor countries with adverse geography don't have sufficient income to invest in the additional infrastructure (such as roads) they need to connect to markets, and since they remain isolated they remain poor. Sachs has also focused attention on the resource curse: poor countries have few economic options other than exporting natural resources, but reliance on natural resources tends to undermine incentives for economic diversification and breed corruption and conflict over control of the resources.[8]

Paul Collier built on the earlier work of Sachs to expand further the idea of traps in his landmark book *The Bottom Billion*. Collier picked up on the geography trap (modifying it slightly as "being landlocked with bad neighbors") and the resource trap and added two more: conflict and bad governance. Low incomes and slow growth make countries more vulnerable to conflict, and conflict keeps countries mired in poverty in a vicious negative cycle. Bad governance keeps countries poor because leaders steal resources and undermine economic opportunities, and poverty itself makes it harder to build the legal, government, and political institutions necessary to improve governance. Collier argues that while it is not impossible for a country to escape these traps, it is tough, and the deck is stacked against them.

In many ways the emerging African countries are beginning to break out of these traps. Two African countries, Botswana and Mauritius, began to emerge in the 1970s, and have continued apace for several decades. For the others, the process began in the late 1980s and early 1990s. The economic policy reforms and political changes initially were followed by a spike in political conflict, but ultimately led to greater stability by the mid-1990s as the changes took hold. From the perspective

---

7 See Jeffrey Sachs et al., "Ending Africa's Poverty Trap," *Brookings Papers on Economic Activity* 1: 117–240; and Jeffrey Sachs, *The End of Poverty: Economic Possibilities for Our Times* (New York: Penguin, 2006).

8 Jeffrey Sachs and Andrew Warner, "Natural Resource Abundance and Economic Growth," National Bureau of Economic Research Working Paper No. W5398 (December 1995). For an earlier exposition of this idea, see Alan Gelb, *Oil Windfalls: Blessing or Curse?* (New York: Oxford University Press, 1988).

of Collier's framework, these political and economic changes began to weaken the grip of the conflict trap, which declined sharply in the late 1990s. With democracy came better leadership and greater accountability, pushed by the new generation of smart activists and entrepreneurs. At the same time, these forces combined to help countries climb out of the bad governance trap. The bankruptcy of past economic approaches and the end of the Cold War discredited extreme forms of socialism, leading to more sensible economic policies. Better economic policies, shrinking debt, and new technologies have helped reduce the reliance on a narrow range of commodity exports and begun to ease the natural resource trap.

South Africa has been an important part of the turnaround. The end of apartheid opened the door for democracy and greater political openness not just in South Africa, but in its neighbors as well. It signaled that democracy and political pluralism could work in Africa, bolstering the confidence of others across the region. And it unleashed an economic engine in which investment and trade were welcomed rather than shunned. Private capital from South Africa has surged into commerce, banking, brewing, and mining in the region. Collier pointed out the perils of having bad neighbors, and South Africa shows what can happen when a neighbor shifts from bad to good. It's no accident that several of South Africa's immediate neighbors are among the emerging countries—

Victoria and Alfred waterfront, Cape Town, South Africa

Botswana, Lesotho, Mozambique, and Namibia—all benefiting from South Africa's revival. Being near South Africa has not guaranteed success—Zimbabwe and Swaziland are two clear exceptions—but the nearby countries that have introduced good economic policies and more democratic governments have leveraged South Africa's turnaround and have thrived since the mid-1990s.

In effect, the five fundamental changes we described above are allowing the emerging countries to begin to break out of these development traps. They have taken the first steps to build the foundation for sustained economic growth, poverty reduction, and improved governance. The early signs are encouraging. Hope for the future has returned in these countries.

But although these fundamental changes are providing countries the opportunity to succeed, there is no guarantee they will do so. These countries are not home free and have not yet permanently broken the bonds of poverty. Far from it. Unfortunately, it is possible that some will slip backward and return to stagnation, or worse.

They face several key risks and challenges, as discussed in the final chapter. Economic management is more complex following the 2008–09 global financial crisis, and as these countries become more integrated in the global economy, they must manage volatility that is beyond their control. But the emerging countries are much better positioned to manage external shocks than they were 30 years ago. They passed a major test during the most recent crisis, in which the downturn was less severe in Africa's emerging countries than in other countries. But their ability to ride out future storms completely is no sure bet; it will require astute economic management and a bit of good luck.

Some countries face the risk of internal political instability. Although the incidence of coups, civil wars, purges, and other conflicts has diminished in these countries, conflict has not completely disappeared, and it could rear its ugly head in response to declining economic prospects or poor policy choices. And while most of the emerging countries have moved far along the path to democracy, several have not come as far and are at more risk of reversal.

Many countries continue to face the ravages of the HIV/AIDS pandemic. And global warming and climate change could destroy nascent economic progress, curtail economic opportunities, and generate political and social tensions that are hard to predict.

And in some countries, it is possible that the early economic progress could simply stall once the earliest and easiest gains are achieved. Sachs, Collier, and others have argued that it was much easier for countries like Mauritius to take advantage of the opportunities afforded by globalization in the 1970s and 1980s when they could diversify into manufacturing with little competition. Today it is much harder, as firms from many more countries compete in global markets, not the least from China and India. But of course there are two sides to that coin. China and India are obviously exporting more, creating competition for potential African exporters. But they are also investing and importing more—a lot more—which creates new opportunities for entrepreneurial African firms to take advantage of Chinese and Indian markets.

There is no denying the risks. They may be too much for some of these countries to overcome. But I believe that there are good reasons to be optimistic that most of the emerging countries will continue their progress and sustain solid economic growth, poverty reduction, and stronger governance.

Doing so surely matters to the 300 million people who live in these countries. It also matters to their neighbors: having economically dynamic and politically stable neighbors is pretty important for any country. And in an increasingly interconnected world, what happens in these countries affects the rest of the world. Strengthening these countries enhances their ability to fight disease, control drug trafficking and other international criminal activity, improve local and regional security, promote economic opportunities, and fight problems that can spread to the rest of the world. And just as important, these countries provide examples for people living in failed and fragile states around the world that there is hope for digging out of poverty and conflict and making progress toward a brighter future.

EMERGING **AFRICA'S**
RENAISSANCE

When Mozambique's civil war ended in 1992, the country was in ruins. Armed rebellion against Portuguese colonial rule had started in the 1960s, but conflict had intensified significantly after the 1974 coup in Lisbon led to Portugal's withdrawal. The new government in Maputo established one-party rule, aligned itself with the Soviet Union, and provided support to the liberation movements in South Africa and Rhodesia, while the governments of South Africa and Rhodesia countered by financing an armed rebellion movement to fight the Mozambican government. Sporadic conflict escalated into all-out war. More than 1 million people died in the conflict, and another 1.7 million became refugees.

Opposite:
Near Ouidah,
Benin

The government's economic approach made a bad situation worse. It nationalized firms, ran large deficits and printed money to finance them, stifled farmers by heavily controlling agricultural prices, and undermined businesses. Investment and trade collapsed, and poverty rates soared. By the early 1990s, Mozambique had become one of the poorest countries in the world. The combination of colonialism, the Cold War, apartheid, mismanagement, and war had created a disaster. Mozambique was a poster child for all that had gone wrong in sub-Saharan Africa.

But all of that changed with the end of the Cold War and apartheid, the cessation of the civil war, the move to democracy, and the introduction of widespread economic reforms. Mozambique held its first multiparty presidential and legislative elections in 1994, and held subsequent elections in 1999, 2004, and 2009. Today, political rights and civil liberties—while far from perfect—are much more widely respected. The government stabilized the economy by cutting the budget deficit, reducing inflation, and improving exchange-rate management to eliminate the black market for currency. It privatized more than 1,200 state-owned enterprises, lowered import tariffs, streamlined customs management, and improved the incentives for farmers. Strong financial support from the donor community helped reduce a crippling debt burden, rebuild roads, schools, and clinics, and otherwise support Mozambique's recovery. The country has attracted significant new investment, led by the Mozal aluminum smelter.

The results have been impressive. Economic growth has averaged 7.5 percent for 15 years, one of the highest growth rates in the world. Average income has *doubled*. Primary school enrollment has jumped from 42 percent to over 70 percent, child mortality has fallen by about 20 percent, and the debt-to-GDP ratio has dropped from 330 percent to 40 percent. Most critical of all, poverty rates have plummeted from 84 percent in 1990 to 64 percent today.

Mozambique is still a poor country and has a long way to go. Poverty, while falling, remains high, especially in rural areas. But the turnaround since the end of the war has been remarkable, marked by more progress than most people could have imagined. The poster child for disaster has become in many ways a model for emerging Africa's economic and political resurgence. And Mozambique is not alone.

Popular Perceptions and Emerging Realities

The popular perception of sub-Saharan Africa is as a region of stagnation, conflict, and authoritarian rule. Journalists, academics, and popular writers continue to depict a continent of little hope or change. Most start with a picture like Figure 2.1, which shows the median income across sub-Saharan Africa since 1960. Commentators typically will either compare the mid-1960s with the mid-1990s or, more recently, compare the mid-1970s with 2000, and proclaim that there has been little change in Africa for 30 or 40 years.

But it's a terribly misleading interpretation, and ever more so as time goes on. For one thing, Figure 2.1 is not a picture of no change—it is a picture of three very distinct phases, each with significant change. First, from about 1960 until about 1977 there was modest growth in median income per capita, from around US$300 to US$350, a rise of about 1 percent per year. Second, from the mid-1970s until the mid-1990s there was a devastating decline, with median income falling back to US$310. This phase encapsulates the continent's well-documented 20-year economic, social, and political collapse.

But as a continent-wide phenomenon, Africa's economic decline ended in 1995, 15 years ago—a point that many commentators cannot seem to

FIGURE 2.1 Changes in Income, Sub-Saharan Africa

Median Real Income per Capita

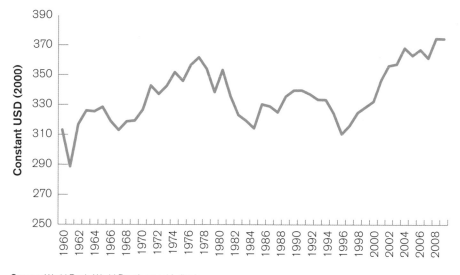

Source: World Bank, World Development Indicators.

grasp.[1] The third phase—and the most meaningful for today—is steady growth since 1995. The median income in SSA rose 20 percent between 1995 and 2008, and is now well above its previous peak.

But the second reason why the popular story is misleading is because the aggregate trend does not capture the variation within the continent, especially during the third phase. We need to dig deeper, because it would be a mistake to suggest that the turnaround since 1995 is shared by all of the countries of sub-Saharan Africa. It is not.

The changes in SSA since the mid-1990s can best be understood by examining three quite different sets of countries (Table 2.1). The first group is oil exporters. Some African oil exporters have recorded rapid growth rates as new discoveries have come online and oil prices have risen. In some cases, this increased income has been accompanied by reductions in poverty and improved social indicators. But in others there has been much less income growth, and in some cases no growth at all, and less improvement in social indicators. Where there has been growth, both its sustainability and the equity of its benefits are major questions. Moreover, as a group the oil exporters have shown relatively

---

1 There are some key exceptions, including Benno Ndulu et al., *The Political Economy of Economic Growth in Africa, 1960–2000*, vols. 1 and 2 (Cambridge: Cambridge University Press, 2008); Edward Miguel, *Africa's Turn?* (Cambridge: MIT Press, 2009); International Monetary Fund, *Regional Economic Outlook: Sub-Saharan Africa* (October 2008); Delfin Go and John Page, eds., *Africa at a Turning Point: Growth, Aid, and External Shocks* (Washington, DC: World Bank, 2008); and Vijay Mahajan, *Africa Rising: How 900 Million African Consumers Offer More Than You Think* (Philadelphia: Wharton School Publishing, 2008). See also Shanta Devarajan's blog, "Africa Can . . . End Poverty," http://blogs.worldbank.org/africacan/.

little change in political rights, civil liberties, democracy, and governance. The relatively poor record of oil-exporting developing countries in recent decades and the volatility of oil prices are cause for strong caution, if not skepticism, in assessing the prospects for this group. I do not judge one way or the other the prospects of these countries or whether recent growth represents the beginnings of deeper and lasting change. For our purposes, I simply recognize that the dynamics in the oil-exporting countries are fundamentally different from those in other countries in Africa, and I do not focus on them other than as an important reference point.

A second group of countries, and the focus of our interest, is the 17 emerging countries, defined (as a starting point) as non–oil exporters that have averaged growth in income per capita of at least 2 percent for 13 years between 1996 and 2008, the last year as of this writing in which full data are available. (I make one exception by including Zambia, even though its 13-year growth rate averaged a slightly lower 1.8 percent because of a poor outcome in 1998. However, its growth averaged 2.3 percent for 10 years between 1999 and 2008). Most of these countries have

TABLE 2.1 Country Groups

Emerging Countries	Other Non–Oil Exporters	Oil Exporters
Botswana	Burundi	Angola
Burkina Faso	Central African Republic	Cameroon
Cape Verde	Comoros	Chad
Ethiopia	Democratic Republic of	Republic of Congo
Ghana	the Congo	Equatorial Guinea
Lesotho	Côte d'Ivoire	Gabon
Mali	Djibouti	Mauritania
Mauritius	Eritrea	Nigeria
Mozambique	The Gambia	Sudan
Namibia	Guinea	
Rwanda	Guinea-Bissau	
São Tomé and Príncipe	Madagascar	
Seychelles	Niger	
South Africa	Somalia	
Tanzania	Swaziland	
Uganda	Togo	
Zambia	Zimbabwe	

Threshold Countries
Benin
Kenya
Liberia
Malawi
Senegal
Sierra Leone

experienced growth even faster than 2 percent, and several have achieved this growth for longer than 13 years. As a group, growth per capita averaged 3.2 percent per year for 13 years, meaning that in these countries *average incomes have increased by 50 percent in real terms since the mid-1990s.* The turnaround in these countries is more than just growth: trade, investment, and private business activity have expanded rapidly; poverty rates have fallen; education and health indicators have improved; and there has been a clear shift toward democracy and stronger governance. But growth provides an informative starting point.

Why 2 percent growth per capita as the basic benchmark? Well, this rate of growth is a common standard in economic analyses indicating reasonably good performance over time. It is approximately equal to the long-term average growth rates of some of today's richest countries, including the United States and the major countries of Europe. It is slightly higher than the global average rate of growth per capita of 1.9 percent per year that has prevailed since 1960. With annual income growth of 2 percent per capita, average incomes double every 36 years, meaning that grandchildren are generally twice as well-off as their grandparents. Two percent growth per capita does not bestow "miracle" performance, but it is a solid benchmark for good performance.

Six additional "threshold" countries fall short of achieving the standard of 2 percent growth per capita for 13 years, but nevertheless have shown signs of beginning a turnaround. Benin, Malawi, and Senegal have all recorded respectable growth rates of between 1.0 and 1.5 percent per year since the mid-1990s—a clear improvement over previous years—and have shown progress on a range of other economic, social, and political indicators. Three other countries started their turnaround more recently. Kenya averaged growth per capita of 2.4 percent between 2003 and 2008 after the end of the 24-year regime of Daniel arap Moi in 2002, although the period was interspersed with intense political volatility, especially in 2007 and 2008. Liberia and Sierra Leone have shown great progress, with rapid economic growth since the end of their conflicts in 2003 and 2002, respectively. Both have become democracies, with marked improvements in political rights, civil liberties, and other measures of democracy and governance.

The third group in our analysis consists of other countries in SSA that have shown relatively little change in income levels, social indicators, and governance. In these countries it is hard to see a fundamental change since the mid-1990s. A few have made some halting progress; others have continued with relatively little change or even retrogression, especially those with continued conflict or those that have experienced little political change.

The differences in economic and political change across these three groups of countries since the mid-1990s make it increasingly difficult to make blanket statements about SSA. And the striking turnaround in the emerging countries makes it impossible to continue to characterize the subcontinent as a region in stagnation or decline. To see these differences over time and across countries more clearly, let's now turn to examining some of the key indicators in more detail.

Growth and Income

Let's begin by looking at the divergence in economic growth and income levels. Until the mid-1990s, there was little difference in the average annual growth rates across the three groups. In all three, the positive growth of the 1960s began to evaporate in the mid-1970s and turned negative in the 1980s (Figure 2.2).

But in the mid-1990s, the pattern changed sharply. In the emerging countries, growth turned positive, jumping above 3 percent on average, where it has remained ever since (with some fluctuation). Growth also increased in the oil exporters, in correspondence with higher prices after 2000. By contrast, growth per capita in the other countries has remained around zero (slightly higher in the most recent years), roughly continuing the pattern of earlier years.

FIGURE 2.2 Growth Has Surged in the Emerging Countries since the mid-1990s
Average Annual Growth in Income per Capita

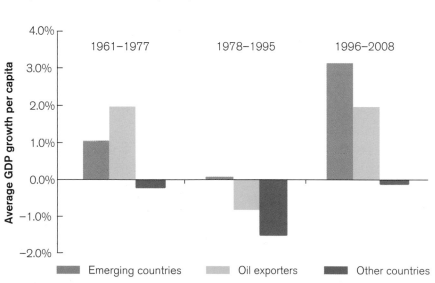

Note: Data for oil exporters exclude Angola and Equatorial Guinea.
Source: World Bank, World Development Indicators Online.

Does this actually represent a real break from the past? Or have we seen this before with other countries in the region? One way to indicate the extent of the change is to examine the number of countries that exceeded 2 percent growth in previous periods. Perhaps in previous periods there were a similar number of fast growers that were offset by others' poor performance and ultimately unable to sustain their initial success. But that is not the case. In the 15-year period from 1980 to 1995, for example, only four non-oil-exporting countries exceeded 2 percent growth: Botswana, Cape Verde, Mauritius, and Swaziland. Even between 1960 and 1977, fewer than 10 countries achieved this mark. With 17 countries now exceeding 2 percent growth, something has clearly changed in a major way since the mid-1990s.[2]

Three percent growth may sound modest, but over 15 years it means a steady rise in incomes for the emerging countries (Figure 2.3). Today, the income per capita in the median emerging country is fully 50 percent higher than in the mid-1990s. By contrast, in the other non-oil-exporting countries, the median income is about the same as in the mid-1990s and remains lower than it was in the mid-1970s.

As shown in Figures 2.2 and 2.3, growth in the emerging countries was already better than in the rest of SSA in the 1980s. Why?

FIGURE 2.3 Sustained Growth Dramatically Raises Incomes

Average Income per Capita

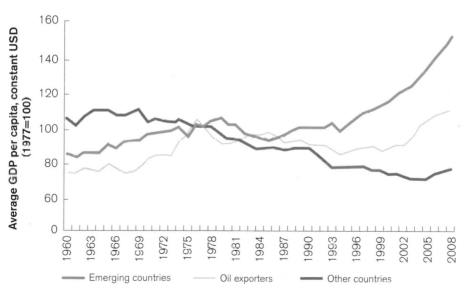

Note: Average for oil exporters excludes Equatorial Guinea.

---

2 For more analysis on growth episodes in SSA, see Go and Page, *Africa at a Turning Point.*

Two answers: Botswana and Mauritius. While the emerging countries as a group began to accelerate economic growth in the mid-1990s, Botswana and Mauritius started much earlier. Long heralded as African success stories, each has a long history of democracy, good governance, and strong economic management. Botswana's growth rate was already relatively high when it gained independence in 1968, but its growth accelerated sharply with the opening of the first diamond mine in 1972. Botswana's income growth per capita has averaged a remarkable 6.3 percent per year for 40 years, one of the fastest sustained growth rates ever recorded in world history. The Mauritian economy initially relied heavily on sugar but began to diversify into textiles, tourism, and other activities in the 1970s and 1980s. The strategy paid off: growth per capita averaged more than 4 percent for two decades, leading to a tripling of average income and significant improvements in a range of social indicators.

The success of Botswana and Mauritius buoyed the average growth rates of the emerging countries, especially in the early periods. With them, the emerging countries averaged zero percent growth per capita between 1977 and 1995, but without them they averaged -0.3 percent growth, similar to the rest of the continent. Botswana and Mauritius have continued their strong performance, but they have affected the average less since 1995 because growth has accelerated in the other emerging countries. With them, the emerging countries averaged growth per capita of 3.2 percent between 1996 and 2008; without them, they averaged 3.1 percent. One way to look at the turnaround in the newer emerging countries is to recognize that they began to follow the examples from Botswana and Mauritius of good governance and more sensible economic policies and are now reaping the benefits.

Critically, the benefits of this growth appear to have been spread relatively equitably. The overall distribution of income actually has improved in the emerging countries, at least according to the Gini coefficient, the most widely used measure of income distribution. The average Gini coefficient (in which a rise indicates worsening inequality) fell from 51.1 in 1993 to 47.7 in 2005 in the emerging countries.

Perhaps most important, poverty rates have fallen markedly. From the early 1980s through the mid-1990s, the share of the population with incomes less than US$1.25 per day hovered around 59 percent. *But since then poverty rates have declined sharply, from 59 percent in 1993 to 48 percent in 2005* (the last year for which data are available), nearly a 20 percent decline in just 12 years.[3]

---

3 World Bank, PovcalNet online database.

Mali is a good example. While under one-party military rule from 1968 to 1991, political rights deteriorated and the economy stagnated. Average income in 1991 was the same as in 1970, and 85 percent of the population lived in absolute poverty. But after protests and riots against the government, the military was forced out of power, and Mali became a multiparty democracy in 1992. The new government began to introduce a program of economic reforms, and with the 1994 devaluation of the CFA franc, the economy began to respond. GDP per capita has grown by a respectable 2.5 percent per year since the mid-1990s, and average income has increased 40 percent. The poverty rate fell sharply to below 60 percent in 2005.

A key reason that the benefits of recent growth have been distributed relatively equitably in many of the emerging countries is that agriculture has been a big part of the turnaround. Agricultural production has been growing at an annual average rate of more than 3.5 percent for 20 years across the emerging countries, meaning that total agricultural production has nearly doubled since 1988 (Figure 2.4). Food production, which for many years grew below population growth rates, is now growing faster than the population, leading to an important increase in food production per capita.

Investment and Trade

Investment and trade have expanded even faster than overall growth. Investment has grown from about 18 percent of GDP in the mid-1980s to over 25 percent of (a much larger) GDP today in the emerging countries. Investment fell sharply in the late 1970s and early 1980s in the emerging countries but began to increase again in the late 1980s following the introduction of economic reforms. It then expanded rapidly in the mid-1990s once the political uncertainty of the early 1990s had given way to more accountable governments. Since 1995, annual investment in the emerging countries has more than doubled in real terms, with investors putting new capital into family farms, large-scale agricultural exports, natural resources, manufacturing, and growing service-sector opportunities (Figure 2.5).

A big part of the increase has come from international investors. Foreign direct investment (FDI) in the emerging countries has jumped from less than 2 percent of GDP to more than 5 percent. In real dollar terms, FDI has more than *quadrupled* in just 13 years. Such investments have ranged from small manufacturers in Ghana, to Celtel's investments in mobile technology across the continent, to new oil palm investments in Libe-

FIGURE 2.4 Agricultural Production is Rising

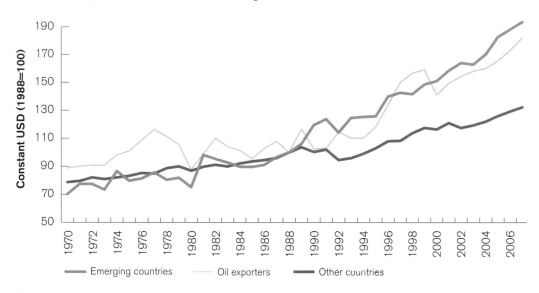

Source: World Bank, World Development Indicators Online.

FIGURE 2.5 Investment Has Soared Since the Mid-1990s

Gross Capital Formation

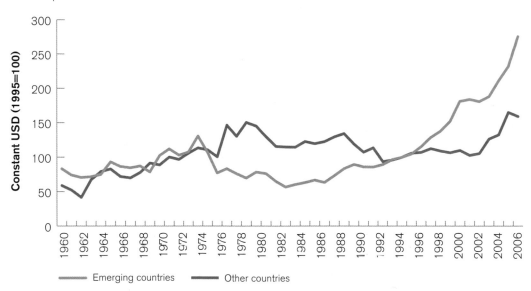

Note: Excludes Rwanda. Oil exporters are excluded because of lack of data.
Source: World Bank, World Development Indicators Online.

ria, to Chinese companies investing in natural resources and infrastructure, to mango exporters in Mali and South Africa, to new power companies across the continent, along with many others.

Consider one small but telling example. In October 2009, a group of 31 businesses from Singapore sent a delegation to explore investment opportunities in Africa, an unthinkable occurrence 15 years ago. "Our firms in sectors such as ports and logistics, environmental services, offshore marine, oil and gas, ICT, urban and infrastructure and commodities are observing new demand patterns. This business mission will help our firms find out more about the promises of the African market," said Lee Yi Shyan, Singapore's Minister of State for Trade & Industry and Manpower, who led the delegation.[4]

Critically, while the amount of investment has increased, the *productivity* of that investment has increased just as sharply. Economists commonly analyze trends in "total factor productivity" (TFP), which broadly captures changes in the productivity of all "factors" of production, including capital, labor, and land. From the mid-1970s through the mid-1990s, TFP growth in the emerging countries fell to zero or became negative as authoritarian governments imposed control regimes that substantially undermined the returns on investment, facilitated corruption, stripped assets, and induced capital flight. In the early 1990s, with the significant instability and uncertainty ushered in by the dramatic economic and political changes of the time, TFP growth was negative, partly because of increases in capital flight as authoritarian leaders reached their last days (Figure 2.6). But as the economic and political situations stabilized in the emerging countries in the mid-1990s, productivity growth began to surge, fluctuated somewhat, and then grew steadily to around 2 percent per year. Meanwhile, in the other countries of SSA, productivity growth has remained negative or near zero.

At the same time, trade has expanded rapidly in the emerging countries. Total trade (exports and imports) rose only gradually from the mid-1980s until the mid-1990s. But since then, trade has far more than doubled (Figure 2.7). Some of the trade is with new partners: Africa's trade with China increased from US$10 billion in 2000 to US$55 billion in 2006. By some estimates, it is expected to reach US$100 billion by 2010.[5] Trade with India and the Middle East has also grown sharply. But much of the trade has grown through expanding relationships with the United States, Europe, and other more traditional partners.

---

4 Diana Othman, "Thirty-one Singapore Firms Head to Africa," *The Straits Times*, October 12, 2009, http://www.straitstimes.com/Breaking+News/Singapore/Story/STIStory_441175.html.

5 Serge Michel and Michel Beuret, *China Safari: On the Trail of Beijing's Expansion in Africa* (New York City: Nation Books, 2009), 3.

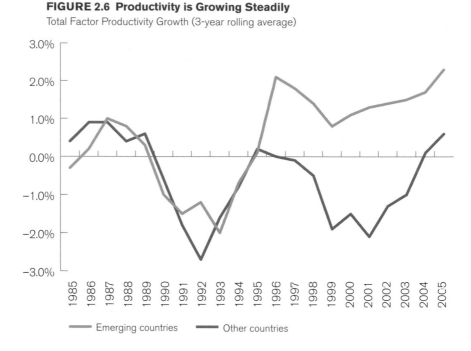

FIGURE 2.6 Productivity is Growing Steadily

Total Factor Productivity Growth (3-year rolling average)

Emerging countries ——— Other countries

Source: Data are drawn from IMF, Regional Economic Outlook, Sub-Saharan Africa, October 2008, p. 30, and provided courtesy of IMF staff.

FIGURE 2.7 Trade Has Tripled

Total Trade (Imports plus exports)

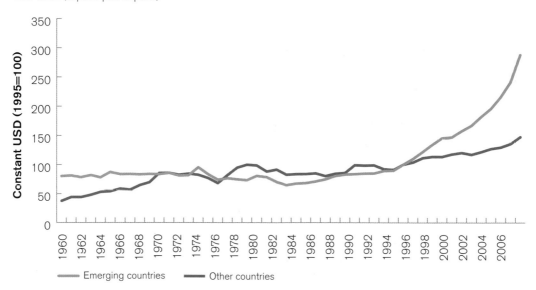

Emerging countries ——— Other countries

Note: Excludes Rwanda and the Democratic Republic of the Congo. Oil Exporters are excluded because of lack of data.

And it has included a wide range of products: fruit, flowers, rubber, wood, aluminum, ore, electricity (exported from Mozambique to South Africa, for example), furniture, jewelry, data entry, and canned tuna, to name a few.

Consider Uganda's exporting of cut flowers, which has grown from essentially nothing 20 years ago to a dynamic sector making significant contributions to employment and exports. In 1992, Uganda's floriculture sector consisted of exactly one two-hectare farm. Today there are more than 20 farms covering nearly 200 hectares. Flower production employs more than 6,000 workers, and annual exports now exceed 5,000 metric tons and US$30 million. Or consider Mali's exports of mangos, which have been growing at around 24 percent per annum since the introduction of new supply-chain management facilities in 2000. Or Zambia's increases in cotton production, or Rwanda's and Cape Verde's rapid increases in tourism. There are many other similar examples of new export activities across the emerging countries.

Education, Health, and Demography

Beyond economics and finance, there have been significant improvements in education, health, and other social indicators. For example, infant mortality rates have come down across the continent, owing to more widespread access to vaccines and life-saving technologies such as oral rehydration therapy. Whereas in 1980 about 93 out of 1,000 children did not live until their first birthday, today the figure is down to about 66 in the emerging countries (Figure 2.8). The pattern of child mortality—the share of children who live to age five—is similar.

There is, unfortunately, a major exception to the generally positive trends in health. The HIV/AIDS pandemic has ravaged families, villages, and cities across Africa, but it has taken an especially heavy toll in southern and central Africa. In Botswana, for example, life expectancy rose rapidly as the country began to progress in the 1970s and 1980s, reaching 63 years in 1987. But then it plummeted to just 46 years in 2002 as the pandemic spread. Fortunately, this pattern has begun to reverse, and life expectancy has begun to climb again, reaching 51 years in 2007. Tragically, several other countries, including South Africa, Lesotho, and Namibia, have followed the pattern of falling life expectancy. In others, life expectancy has not fallen as sharply, but improvements have stalled. Recent efforts to combat HIV/AIDS by individuals, communities, governments, and the international community have begun to have some initial impact, but there is a long way to go.

FIGURE 2.8 Infant Mortality Rates Are Declining across SSA

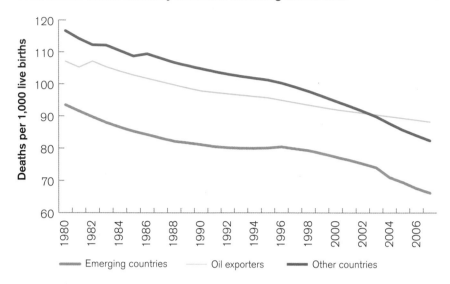

Source: UNICEF Statistics, http://www.unicef.org/statistics/index_24302.html accessed September 15, 2009.

Nevertheless, with this huge exception, there has been significant progress on a range of health indicators during the last decade. In Rwanda, for example, the government has introduced an aggressive strategy to strengthen the health sector and has achieved impressive results. It implemented a performance-based funding system in which its funding to local facilities depends on the progress they achieve on specific goals. It decentralized management, allowing facilities to make decisions on hiring, firing, and wages, and scaled up a community-based insurance program. It took strong steps to improve the coordination and harmonization of donor flows through direct budget support and a pooled fund of resources for the health sector. It increased public funding for health and attracted much larger funds from donors so that funding for health per capita soared from a meager US$3 in 1998 to US$33 in 2008.[6] The turnaround has been remarkable. Infant mortality rates dropped from 130 per 1,000 in 1998 to 75 in 2007, and maternal mortality rates from nearly 1,100 per 100,000 to 750 over the same period, partly because the share of assisted births rose from one-third to one-half. Malaria incidence is down by two-thirds.[7] There is still far to go for Rwanda to achieve all of its health goals, but it has made an impressive start.

---

6 World Bank, Program Document on Rwanda First Community Living Standards Grant (March 2, 2009), http://go.worldbank.org/6HEPNT1OB0.

FIGURE 2.9 Population Growth Rates Have Begun to Decline

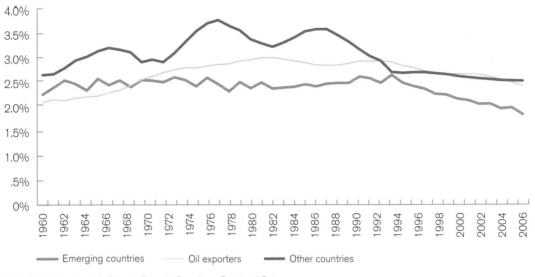

Note: Data do not include Djibouti, Rwanda, Somalia, or Equatorial Guinea.
Source: World Bank, World Development Indicators.

At the same time, there have been major reductions in both fertility rates and population growth rates across most of SSA. Fertility rates have dropped from the extraordinarily high levels of 6.6 births per woman or even higher in the 1960s and 1970s to less than 5 today. In the emerging countries, fertility rates now average 4.5 births per woman, down from 6.6 in 1975. Similarly, population growth rates in the emerging countries reached 2.6 percent in the early 1990s. But since 1995, they have dropped steadily (Figure 2.9). By 2006, just 11 years later, the average population growth rate had dropped below 2 percent in the emerging countries.

Turning to education, primary school enrollment rates have risen steadily and now average 80 percent in the emerging countries. This translates to millions more kids in school every year. Critically, a far larger share is now completing primary school. Although reliable information over time on school completion rates is hard to come by, for 13 of the emerging countries for which data are available for the last decade, the change is clear. In these countries, about 63 percent of children were completing primary school in 1998–99, but by 2007 the share had jumped to 72 percent. By comparison, the average comple-

---

7 Claude Sekabaraga, "Rwanda Performance Based System. Public Reforms," Rwanda Ministry of Health, http://www.slideshare.net/RikuE/rwanda-performance-based-system-public-refoms-presentation.

tion rate in other SSA countries is about 55 percent. That is, in the emerging countries, nearly three out of four children are now completing primary school, and the rate is growing quickly. There is still much work to do to increase the completion rate and improve the quality of education, but this is a welcome step that bodes well for the future.

Consider the recent changes in Tanzania. The country's education programs steadily deteriorated in the 1980s and 1990s. By 2000, primary school enrollment rates were just 53 percent, and only about half of primary school–age children were completing school. Those who did were not getting a very good education—only 22 percent passed the final primary school national exam. But in 2001 the government eliminated school fees, paving the way for much greater participation. At the same time, it aggressively recruited more qualified teachers, strengthened teacher training, made more school books available, and took other steps to improve quality. Primary school enrollments are now over 90 percent, meaning more than 2 million additional children are in school. School retention and completion have also increased substantially, with the primary school completion rate reaching 85 percent in 2007. The quality of education also seems to be improving, with the share of students passing national exams growing to 62 percent in 2006.[8] There are still many challenges, but Tanzania has clearly taken the critical first steps in building a much stronger education system, a process that is beginning in many other countries across the subcontinent.

The Millennium Development Goals

The emerging countries are also making steady progress toward achieving the Millennium Development Goals (MDGs). The MDGs are a series of development targets, established at a United Nations conference in 2000, that countries are aiming to meet by 2015.[9] There are eight main goals (seven for developing countries and one that measures the support provided by donor countries) ranging from halving poverty to halting the spread of HIV/AIDS to providing universal primary education. According to an analysis by Ben Leo of the Center for Global Development, Africa's emerging countries are making much greater progress

---

8 Data on school enrollment and completion rates are from the World Development Indicators. Data on exam pass rates from the World Bank, "Supporting Education in Tanzania," http://go.worldbank.org/U1Q0BYXKW0.

9 For more background see http://www.un.org/millenniumgoals/.

achieving the goals than other countries in Africa. Thirteen of the seventeen emerging countries are on track to achieve at least half the MDGs by 2015, compared to only three of the nine oil exporters and just 3 out of 16 of the other SSA countries. The emerging countries are on track to achieve an average of 3.8 of 8 goals, compared to 2.8 in the oil exporters, and just 2.2 for the other countries.[10] Several emerging countries have made particularly significant progress, including Burkina Faso, Cape Verde, Ethiopia, Ghana, and Uganda.

Commodity Prices

One plausible explanation for the economic turnaround in the emerging countries is favorable commodity prices. In recent years, prices for a range of commodities exported by these countries have risen. For example, both gold and coffee prices have tripled since 2001. Copper prices have quadrupled, and timber prices have nearly doubled. There is no doubt that favorable prices have attracted investment and helped spur production in these sectors. They have clearly contributed to growth in several countries, at least since 2001 or 2002.

But export prices alone are too simple an explanation for the turnaround in the emerging countries. The increases in many export prices began in 2001, whereas the economic turnaround in the emerging countries started in the mid-1990s. And in the late 1990s, the opposite was true: export prices were falling as world demand softened during the Asian financial crisis. The emerging countries began to grow in the mid-1990s *despite* the fall in export prices.

Moreover, although export prices have risen since 2001, import prices have risen by even more in most countries. In particular, the spike in oil and food prices in recent years has raised production prices and worked against economic growth in the emerging countries (all of which are net oil importers). One way to see the overall impact of trade prices is through the net barter terms of trade, which measure the ratio of export prices to import prices, as shown in Figure 2.10. Overall, the average terms of trade for the emerging countries declined steadily throughout the 1990s before leveling off and rebounding around 2005. That is, for most of the period of rapid growth since 1995 in the emerging countries, the terms of trade have worked *against* them. Thus, while commodity prices have helped in

10 Data provided by Ben Leo. His analysis examines eight indicators corresponding to the first 7 MDGs (for MDG1, he examines two indicators, the share of the population below the poverty line and the prevalence of underweight children). See Benjamin Leo and Julia Barmeier, "Who Are the MDG Trailblazers? A New MDG Progress Index," CGD Working Paper, forthcoming.

FIGURE 2.10 Commodity Prices Are Not the Main Force behind the Growth in the Emerging Countries

Net barter terms of trade (ratio of export prices to import prices)

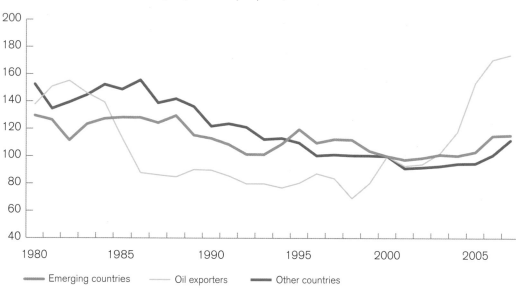

Source: World Bank, World Development Indicators Online.

some cases, the turnaround in the emerging countries is not solely the result of favorable commodity prices.

❋ ❋ ❋

Across the emerging countries, the pattern since the mid-1990s is clear. Income, agricultural production, trade, investment, health, and education are all up. Poverty is down. Yes, many flaws remain, both economically and politically, and the changes have not been as far-reaching or as fast as some might have hoped. But the break from the past is unmistakable. These countries look much different today than in the mid-1990s.

There is reason to believe the break from the past can be expanded and sustained. Specifically, as introduced in the first chapter, five major changes are under way in these countries: (1) the movement toward more democratic and accountable governments; (2) the shift to more sensible economic policies; (3) the end of the debt crisis and changing partner relationships; (4) the spread of new technologies; and (5) the emergence of a new generation of political, economic, and social leaders. Again, the first two changes ignited the economic re-

---

11 For a thoughtful discussion of the turnaround in Africa, see Miguel, *Africa's Turn*? (n. 1).

naissance in the mid-1990s and the next three and have helped sustain the turnaround. Collectively, they provide the basis for understanding why the economic stagnation and decline that characterized these countries has turned to steady progress and growth. More important, they provide the foundation for a brighter future in which these countries can continue to make progress in the years to come.

The chapters that follow explore each of these five changes in more depth.

EMERGING
DEMOCRACIES

On November 8, 1989, the people of Namibia quietly started a revolution. For five days, they turned out in droves to line up for hours under the broiling sun to do something that they, their parents, and their grandparents had not been allowed to do: peacefully and openly choose their national leaders. An amazing 98 percent of registered voters turned out to elect 72 delegates to a constituent assembly that would draft a new constitution that would later lead to presidential elections and the formation of a new government.[1] Little did they know that their actions would reverberate far beyond their borders and mark the beginning of a slow but steady sweep of democracy across Africa.

And little did they know that exactly as they were voting, far away from their country, forces were under way that would bring about some of the most important political changes in world history. Five thousand miles away in Berlin, the very next day on November 9, the government of East Germany hurriedly opened many of the checkpoints dividing East and West Germany. The Berlin Wall was about to fall. Political relationships and systems around the world were about to undergo seismic changes, most obviously in Eastern Europe, but also in Namibia and in many countries across sub-Saharan Africa that had been under the long shadow of the Cold War. But it was not just the Cold War. Just nine weeks later on February 11, 1990, South Africa released Nelson Mandela from jail. Apartheid was beginning to crumble as well.

Namibia's elections were a long time coming. Germany's colonial occupation of the territory, known then as South West Africa, had ended

Opposite:

Liberian woman casts her ballot in the 2005 presidential election (©2010 Benjamin Spatz)

---

1 Christopher Wren, "Milestone in Africa: Namibians Vote their Future," *New York Times,* November 8, 1989, http://www.nytimes.com/1989/11/08/world/milestone-in-africa-namibians-vote-their-future.html.

EMERGING DEMOCRACIES **47**

along with World War I. But South Africa's apartheid government took control, initially under a League of Nations mandate that lasted until 1946. When the League of Nations was dissolved in 1946, the newly formed United Nations pushed to end South Africa's rule and place South West Africa under a UN trusteeship. But South Africa refused to cooperate; instead it unilaterally and illegally annexed the territory.

In the mid-1960s, armed conflict began along the border with Angola between South African troops on the one side and the military wing of the South West Africa People's Organization (SWAPO) on the other, supported by Angola and later Cuba. The South African Border War, as it came to be known, mixed apartheid with the Cold War in an ugly combination. The United States provided covert support to South Africa, while Russia, Cuba, and Angola all supported SWAPO. The war lasted more than 20 years.

Finally, in late 1988, South Africa, Angola, and Cuba agreed to a regional peace accord in a pact mediated by the United States, with the Soviet Union as an official observer. The agreement linked the withdrawal of South African troops and Namibian independence to the end of Soviet military aid and the withdrawal of Cuban troops from Angola.

It also paved the way for the historic 1989 elections. Namibian independence followed shortly thereafter on March 21, 1990. After decades of struggle—both violent and peaceful—Namibians finally could speak for themselves. Voters rode on crammed trucks, pedaled bicycles, or walked for hours through the bush just to vote.

> "They feel like human beings," said the Rev. Liborius Ndumbu, an Ovambo priest at the Roman Catholic mission in the nearby settlement of Anamulenge.
>
> "They have got rights; they are voting for the future of the country. . . . It is very exciting for them." . . .
>
> "My dream has been fulfilled." [2]

The elections hardly solved all of Namibia's problems and by themselves were no guarantee of democracy, accountability, better governance, or increased prosperity. Elections, even fair ones, are not the same as democracy. The process of democratization is rarely smooth and does not happen all at once, and Namibia was no exception. Since independence, there have been conflicts and controversies over land reform, human rights, and President Sam Nujoma's decision to run for a third term in 1999, among many other issues. But over time, Namibia's democracy has

---

2 Christopher Wren, "Namibian Voting is Eager and Heavy," *New York Times,* November 11, 1989, http://www.nytimes.com/1989/11/11/world/namibian-voting-is-heavy-and-eager.html.

continued to mature and solidify. Mr. Nujoma stepped down in 2005, and Namibians elected Hifikepunye Pohamba as their second president. Namibia now ranks relatively high in observance of civil liberties, political rights, and other similar indicators.

Namibia's 1989 election was enormously important in its own right, but its significance spread well beyond the territory's borders. Although it was not obvious at the time, a new era of democracy in sub-Saharan Africa—fragile, imperfect, and uncertain—had begun.

The Rise of the Big Man

Fifty years ago, as the great wave of independence movements swept across Africa, there was enormous hope for democracy and for competent, accountable governments. Citizens fully anticipated that the new governments would reverse the dictatorial practices of the colonial rulers and instead would work on behalf of all citizens to bring prosperity and development. Many independence leaders pledged to protect political freedoms and civil liberties and introduced constitutions that enshrined political pluralism. In some cases, the beginnings of competitive multiparty political systems began to emerge.

But once the initial post-independence leaders were installed, many quickly moved to seize full control. Nascent pluralistic systems gave way to authoritarianism and military rule. Power became concentrated in strong executives, with weak judicial and legislative branches easily co-opted to go along. Authoritarian governments allowed little dissent. They curtailed civil liberties and political freedoms, outlawed opposition parties, seized control of the press, weakened auditing and other public financial control mechanisms, and dismantled the few remaining institutions of restraint and checks on power.[3]

By the mid-1980s, in the years just before the dramatic changes in Namibia, almost every sub-Saharan African country was ruled by a dictator. The era of the African "big man" was at its zenith.[4] General Ibrahim Babangida was in the midst of his reign as president of the Armed Forces Ruling Council of Nigeria, with the tyrannical rule of Sani Abacha not to begin for several more years. Samuel Doe's disastrous dictatorship in Liberia had several more years to run before it would come to a bloody end, only to be replaced by 14 years of civil war dominated by the even worse Charles Taylor. Mobutu Sese Seko was two decades into his oppressive rule in Zaire. And the list went on.

---

3 See Paul Collier, "Africa's External Relations, 1960–1990," *African Affairs* 90(3): 339–56.

4 For a good discussion of Africa's "big men," see Todd Moss, *African Development: Making Sense of the Issues and Actors* (Boulder, CO: Lynne Rienner Publishers, 2007).

Democracy was rare. Few countries met even minimum standards for democracies in terms of protecting fundamental political freedoms and civil liberties, or in establishing key institutions such as free and fair elections, representative government, and checks on executive power. This was evident in any of a wide variety of measures of democracy, such as Freedom House's *Freedom in the World* index and the University of Maryland / George Mason University *Polity IV Index of Political Regime Characteristics and Transitions* (see Box 3.1, page 68). Of the 48 countries in SSA, only three met basic standards of democracy captured by both of these indices in the mid-1980s: Botswana, The Gambia, and Mauritius. And The Gambia was soon to fall prey to a 1994 coup d'état, ending more than 25 years of democratic leadership.

Outside of these countries, most leaders weren't even bothering with a façade of democracy, much less the deeper substance of accountability to their citizenry. From 1985 through 1989, the five years preceding Namibia's election, competitive elections (in which an opposition party gained some presence in the national legislature) were held in just nine African countries.[5] Governance was dominated by strong-man presidents who faced few constraints on power—other than the threat of violent overthrow—and who could easily ignore inconvenient constitutional restrictions and laws with impunity.

The strong political hand was matched by a strong economic hand. Buttressed by the powerful currents of global ideologies of the 1960s and 1970s, most governments introduced wide-ranging state controls over the economy, including fixing exchange rates and interest rates, regulating a vast array of prices, running business empires extending from power companies to corner grocery stores, subsidizing favored private businesses, expanding the civil service, and introducing controls on imports and exports. These policies, dubbed as "control regimes" by the AERC Africa growth study, were at the heart of the downward economic spiral that began in the mid-1970s, as discussed in Chapter 4.

The political and economic systems were deeply intertwined. In the absence of competitive and accountable political systems, authoritarian governments had little need to implement policies that would benefit the majority of citizens; they instead funneled economic benefits to their key supporters: civil servants, protected businesses, labor unions, the military, and urban consumers. Farmers and others with little political clout were particularly vulnerable to losing out. Political scientist Robert Bates has demonstrated the link statistically: authoritarian governments in SSA, whether one-party states or military regimes, were far more likely to

---

5 Michael Bratton and Nicolas van de Walle, *Democratic Experiments in Africa: Regime Transitions in Comparative Perspective* (Cambridge: Cambridge University Press, 1997), 7.

maintain strong economic control regimes than less authoritarian governments.[6] Whereas in other regions of the world, especially Asia, the relationship between authoritarianism and economic performance is ambiguous, in SSA it is clear: with few exceptions, authoritarian governments have had disastrous economic records.

And so it was that in the 1980s, as authoritarian governments tightened their grip, economic performance plummeted precipitously. Africa's development crisis was in full swing.

The Forces of Change

Strong political and economic controls enabled many governments to maintain power for years, and in some cases decades, but these systems contained the seeds of their own ultimate destruction. The economic dynamics proved unsustainable, especially following the global oil shocks of the mid-1970s. As the world economy stalled, budget and trade deficits ballooned across SSA, investment declined, and capital fled. To finance the deficits, governments borrowed from abroad and printed money at home, generating both large debts and rising inflation. But once Mexico defaulted on its debts in August 1982, bank credit for African countries almost completely disappeared. Governments were forced to borrow at home from local banks and suppliers, but there wasn't much to borrow. Financing options were disappearing fast.

By the mid-1980s, many governments were running out of room to maneuver. Without financing, there was little choice: deficits had to be closed. And this meant painful choices to cut spending, reduce subsidies on food and fuel, cut health and education services, raise taxes, and devalue currencies. Governments were forced to turn to the International Monetary Fund to obtain emergency funding and debt rescheduling in return for adopting stringent reform programs. Although these reform programs—always controversial because of the tough austerity measures and struggles over the role of states and markets that are their core—generally succeeded in their immediate aim of closing deficits and bringing about some degree of macroeconomic stability, they did so at a cost, both economically and politically. And they had little impact, at least initially, on stimulating economic growth and creating clear benefits for most citizens. The economic benefits only accrued later.

But the austerity measures immediately and directly threatened the economic interests of the key beneficiaries of authoritarian rule. Civil ser-

---

6   Robert Bates, "Domestic Interests and Control Regimes," in *The Political Economy of Economic Growth in Africa, 1960–2000,* vol. 1, ed. Ndulu, et al. (Cambridge: Cambridge University Press, 2008), 185.

vants and union workers saw their pay cut or their jobs disappear. Urban consumers, including the military, watched electricity, food, and fuel prices rise and had to pay steep black-market premiums for scarce foreign currency. Protected businesses lost their subsidies and tariff protection.

Authoritarian governments in SSA had seen protests before. But in the past, they had always been able to respond to them by raising civil service wages, cutting university tuitions, or increasing subsidies for food or electricity. No more. As Bates put it, "Authoritarian governments appear to have fallen not because they faced more unrest but because they were unable to respond to it."[7] Many of the very groups that had supported authoritarian governments now turned on them. By the late 1980s, political protests were on the rise, often starting with university students and spreading to labor unions, civil servants, and other groups. The number of protests across the continent rose from fewer than 20 per year in the early 1980s to more than 50 in 1990, and continued to rise to more than 80 in both 1991 and 1992.[8]

The discontent was rooted in more than just lost economic benefits for the favored few—it was much more widespread. Basic beliefs, ideas, and opinions were changing as well.[9] Increasingly, civic leaders, bankers, economists, religious clergy, business leaders, and others in the intellectual elite began to recognize the failures of the past and to call for political and economic change. It was increasingly evident to them that, despite the claims of their leaders, the old systems were economically, intellectually, and politically bankrupt, as political scientists Michael Bratton and Nicolas van de Walle observed:

> In previous years, rewards and repression had served to quell unrest. Not so in the 1990s. Spurred by deepening economic distress and reacting against heavy-handed government tactics, protestors began to insist on political change. For the first time, narrow economic interests were superseded by calls for the ejection of national leaders and the reintroduction of plural politics.[10]

As these domestic forces led the way for change, international pressures pushed in the same direction.[11] Donor policies played a role, although they were secondary to other forces. Donors increasingly condi-

---

7 Robert Bates, "Political Reform," in *The Political Economy of Economic Growth in Africa, 1960–2000,* vol. 1, ed. Ndulu, et al. (Cambridge: Cambridge University Press, 2008), 363.

8 Bratton and Van de Walle, *Democratic Experiments,* 3, 100.

9 Benno Ndulu, "The Evolution of Global Development Paradigms and Their Influence on African Economic Growth," in *The Political Economy of Economic Growth in Africa, 1960–2000,* vol. 1, ed. Ndulu, et al. (Cambridge: Cambridge University Press, 2008), chapter 9.

10 Bratton and Van de Walle, *Democratic Experiments,* 104.

11 For a more in-depth discussion of the domestic and international forces behind political reform in Africa, see Bates, "Political Reform," and Bratton and Van de Walle, *Democratic Experiments.*

tioned their financial support on countries' adopting stabilization policies and moving away from controlled economies and toward more open markets, especially after the election of the Reagan and Thatcher governments in the United States and United Kingdom. While some countries became adept at avoiding these conditions (and many of the conditions were poorly designed), the shifting global consensus away from a strong economic role for the state and toward more flexible markets began to gain more widespread traction.

The most powerful international forces were the end of the Cold War and, alongside it, the demise of apartheid. As global power structures began to change, many authoritarian governments lost their patrons, eliminating both their financing options and the last remnants of their international legitimacy. Authoritarian governments could no longer turn to their old friends to bail them out with no questions asked. Economically, strong forms of socialism and state control lost credibility. Politically, growing calls for more pluralistic and competitive governments in Eastern and Central Europe were heard around the world, giving confidence and inspiration to protest groups across Africa.

On New Year's Eve in 1989, Frederick Chiluba, Chairman of the Zambia Congress of Trade Unions (and future president of Zambia), asked at a labor rally, "If the owners of socialism have withdrawn from the one-party system, who are the Africans to continue with it?" The next day in Nairobi, Kenya, the Reverend Timothy Njoya of the Presbyterian Church of East Africa used a New Year's Day sermon to argue that if one-party ideologies were collapsing in Eastern Europe, African governments also should shift toward democracy.[12] African citizens were not just angry. Now they were emboldened.

Changes began to unfurl rapidly in the late 1980s and early 1990s, at least in many countries. The sequence of events varied across countries, and of course in some countries there was little change at all. But a general pattern began to emerge. The austerity measures of the mid-1980s were followed by a rise in political protests, which, according to a careful analysis by Bratton and Van de Walle, peaked in 1991.[13] Many governments responded to the protests by beginning to introduce reforms to guarantee civil liberties, which reached an initial peak in 1992. This was followed by an upswing in competitive political elections, which rose from no more than 2 per year in the 1980s to 14 in 1993. Almost in tandem, governments began to adhere to greater political rights, which surged to an initial peak

12 As cited in Bratton and Van de Walle, *Democratic Experiments,* 105.
13 Ibid., 3–6.

in 1994, the year that Nelson Mandela rose to the presidency of South Africa.

The push toward democracy was on.

The Spread of Democracy, 1989–2008

Today, just two decades after Namibia's historic elections, the political landscape has changed dramatically. Using the Freedom House and Polity IV indicators, the number of democracies in SSA rose from 3 in 1989 to 23 in 2008 (Figure 3.1). Following Namibia, the change began in earnest in 1991—the year of the dissolution of the Soviet Union—when Benin, Cape Verde, Comoros, Madagascar, São Tomé and Príncipe, and Zambia all began to shift toward democracy. In South Africa, the end of apartheid in 1994 ushered in a new era across the southern region of the continent. By 1994, Lesotho, Mozambique, Malawi, and South Africa had joined the ranks of the new democracies.

In the early years, the changes were rapid. According to Bratton and Van de Walle, between 1990 and 1994, 38 African countries held competitive elections—quadrupling the number of the previous five years—and the average share of legislative seats held by opposition parties tripled from 10 to 31 percent. They count 29 of the 38 as "founding" elections, meaning that the position of head of government was openly contested following a period in which political competition had been denied. Eleven sitting

FIGURE 3.1 The Rise of Democracy in Africa

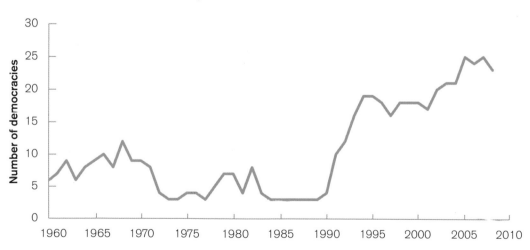

Source: Author's calculations, based on the methodology and sources described in Box 3.1. To count as a democracy, a country must score four or less on the average Freedom House index *and* zero or greater on the polity index from Polity IV.

presidents were voted out of office during that first flurry of elections, with Benin's Kerekou the first to go. Three more presidents decided not to seek re-election.[14] An unmistakable change was under way.

But by the mid-1990s, there were worries that democratization in SSA had stalled or even was beginning to erode. Between 1994 and 1999, only Ghana joined the ranks of emerging democracies, and several countries took steps backward, including Comoros, the Republic of Congo (Brazzaville), The Gambia, Niger, and Zambia.

But the death of Nigeria's brutal dictator Sani Abacha in June 1998 led to the election of Olusegun Obasanjo the following year and launched Nigeria's fragile and incomplete move toward democracy. Ghana held elections in 1992 and 1996 and solidified its change in 2000 when it elected an opposition candidate, John Kufuor, to succeed Jerry Rawlings. It repeated the process in a very close, well-run, and peaceful election in early 2009 by electing opposition candidate John Atta Mills (Rawling's former vice president) to succeed Kufuor. By 2002, Kenya, Senegal, Sierra Leone, and Zambia had joined the ranks. And the end of the civil war in Liberia ushered in a new era of democracy with the elections of October 2005, in which Ellen Johnson Sirleaf became the first woman elected head of state in Africa.

This change is remarkable: in just 20 years, Africa has gone from almost no democracies to nearly half the continent under democratic rule. It is all the more extraordinary because so many of the countries are among the poorest in the world, and it was long thought that democracy wasn't really feasible for low-income countries. Yet when Mozambique became a democracy in 1994, it had an income per capita of just US$130, making it one of the poorest countries in the world. Of SSA's 23 democracies, 12 have incomes per capita below US$600. *Never before in history have so many low-income countries become democracies in so short a time.*

The shift toward popularly elected governments in these countries was a watershed achievement. Consider the account in the *New York Times* of Sierra Leone's 2002 elections following a decade of brutal war:

> On Election Day in Sierra Leone, the exhilaration was palpable at a camp for those with hacked-off limbs, the injuries that defined the horrors of that country's civil war. Among them was Lamine Jusu Jarka, whose hands were cut off in a rebel attack in 1999. Mr. Jarka voted by stamping his ballot sheet with an ink-stained toe. "This morning, I am voting for the future," he said. [15]

---

14 Ibid., 7, 197.

15 Rachel Swarns and Norimitsu Onishi, "Africa Creeps Along Path to Democracy," *New York Times*, June 2, 2002, http://www.nytimes.com/2002/06/02/world/africa-creeps-along-path-to-democracy. html.

The dramatic changes in political competitiveness have been most evident in the executive branch of power, but to some extent have extended
to legislatures, as shown in Table 3.1, panels a and b, respectively. With
respect to the executive, 36 of 46 countries in 1990 had an executive that
was either unelected or elected in a contest with only one candidate. By
2006, there had been nearly a complete flip, and only nine leaders were
chosen that way; in 36 countries, multiple parties competed and won
votes, and the winner received less than 75 percent of the votes. A similar
pattern of change is evident in legislative contests. In 1990, 35 countries
had no legislature, an unelected one, or an elected one with only one party. By 2006, only six legislatures had those characteristics. Instead, 37 legislatures included multiple parties, with the largest party receiving less
than 75 percent of the vote. Competitive politics had arrived in SSA.

TABLE 3.1 Politics Have Become More Competitive in Sub-Saharan Africa

Score	Description	No. of countries	
		1990	2006
a. Executive index of political competitiveness, SSA			
7	The largest party received less than 75 percent of the votes	7	23
6	Multiple parties competed and won votes [a]	1	13
5	Multiple parties are legal, but only one won votes [b]	0	0
4	One party, multiple candidates	0	0
3	Elected, one candidate	20	5
2	Unelected executive	16	4
1	No executive	0	0
	N/A	2	1
b. Legislative index of political competitiveness, SSA			
7	The largest party received less than 75 percent of the seats	3	29
6	Multiple parties competed and won seats [a]	6	8
5	Multiple parties are legal, but only one won seats [b]	0	2
4	One party, multiple candidates	16	1
3	Elected, one candidate	7	1
2	Unelected legislature	2	2
1	No legislature	10	2
	N/A	2	1

a But one party won 75 percent or more of the seats.
b Because other parties did not exist, compete, or win seats.

Source: World Bank, Database of Political Institutions (updated 2010), http://go.worldbank.org/2EAGGLRZ40. See Thorsten
Beck, et al., "New Tools in Comparative Political Economy: The Database of Political Institutions," *World Bank Economic Review*
15(1): 165–176.

But elections alone do not make democracies. Democracy requires the protection of basic civil liberties and human rights; the establishment of public institutions that are accountable to their citizens and that limit the power of their leaders; and the recognition of rights of freedom of expression, assembly, and the press, among other dimensions. These changes do not come about overnight, nor do they follow automatically from elections.

But they are beginning to happen in Africa—slowly, unevenly, imperfectly, but unmistakably—alongside freer and fairer elections. Three key developments stand out in the shift to democratic governance.

1. **There is a clear shift away from the politics of the individual big man toward institutionalization of power and adherence to basic rules of the game.**

The formal institutions and rules that had been so easily ignored in the past are beginning to matter in many countries. Political scientists Daniel Posner and Daniel Young have pointed out that from the 1960s through the 1980s the vast majority of African rulers left office through some form of violent overthrow, but since 1990 the reverse is true. The majority leave office through elections, resignations, or other institutionalized processes. More specifically, between 1960 and 1980 nearly three-quarters of African leaders left office through violent overthrow or assassination—more than three times the global average—whereas between 2000 and 2005 only one out of five succumbed to violent overthrows, about equal to the global average (Figure 3.2).[16]

Furthermore, Posner and Young point out that, more than ever before, new leaders face far greater constraints that limit them from keeping power indefinitely. More countries now constitutionally limit the president to two terms in power, and term limits are more likely to be honored and attempts to circumvent them more likely to fail, especially in the democracies. Since 1990, only one country among SSA's 23 democracies—Namibia—has successfully amended a constitution to allow a third term (there were only five other such amendments among SSA's nondemocracies). By contrast, in 15 cases term limits were honored, either because there was no attempt to amend the constitution (12 cases) or the attempt to do so was unsuccessful (3 cases).[17]

---

16 Daniel N. Posner and Daniel J. Young, "The Institutionalization of Political Power in Africa," *Journal of Democracy* 18(3): 126–140.

17 Ibid., 132. Posner and Young list nine countries that had no attempt to amend the constitution, but they restrict their analysis to countries that adopted new constitutions after 1990. In addition to their list, Botswana, Mauritius, and South Africa have honored term limits.

FIGURE 3.2 Political Leadership Change: Coups are Out, Elections are In
Manner of Departure from Power as Share of All Transitions

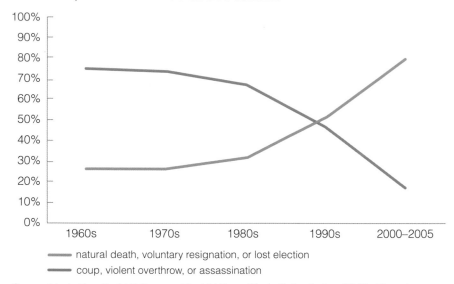

Source: Adapted from Daniel N. Posner and Daniel J. Young, "The Institutionalization of Political Power in Africa," *Journal of Democracy* 18(3): 128.

In addition, legislatures and other government institutions of restraint such as court systems, local governments, and electoral commissions are slowly growing stronger. As political scientist Joel Barkan has observed, "Once the rubber stamp of the executive, or non-existent during periods of military rule, [African legislatures] have begun to assert their independence as players in the policymaking progress, as watchdogs of the executive, and as organizations that respond to the demands of civil society."[18] African legislatures remain weak in relation to the executive, but are much stronger today than they were 15 years ago, and they are increasingly important players in setting policy agendas and restraining the power of presidents and chief executives.

2. There have been substantial improvements in the extent to which civil liberties and political rights are honored and enforced.

Governments are much more likely to support basic rights of freedom of speech, the press, and assembly, alongside other basic civil liberties and political rights. In today's 23 democracies, the Freedom House scores on the protection of civil liberties (on a scale of 1 to 7, with 1 the best and 7 the worst) improved substantially, from an average score of 4.9 in 1990 to 2.8 in 2008. In some countries the change was even more dramatic: Ghana, for example, recorded a dismal 6 in 1991, but today its score is 1.5. The improve-

---

18 Joel Barkan, "African Legislatures and the 'Third Wave' of Democratization," in *Legislative Power in Emerging African Democracies*, ed. Joel Barkan (Boulder, CO: Lynne Rienner, 2009), 1.

ment in the protection of political rights across all these countries was even larger, with the average score improving from 5.2 in 1990 to 2.7 in 2008.

In many countries, people are beginning to see change with respect to basic rights, as captured by this sentiment following the 2002 elections in Mali:

> "Justice prevails a little more," said Sulamo Djiguiba, a wizened old man who was contemplating democracy on Election Day. "During the military regime, soldiers would just come and arrest us and make us work for the army or on their farms. Now that doesn't exist. We are free. We can go where we like." Ansema Djiguiba, 25, agreed. "The mayor and his representatives come and we have the right to talk about our needs without fear," he said. "They have dug wells for us. Some villages have schools. But we are still asking for more help. Many people are still hungry." [19]

In addition to civil liberties and political rights, a wide range of other governance indicators have significantly improved, as we explore later in this chapter. The press in the emerging democracies is much more active, with far more radio, newspaper, magazine, television, and internet outlets. The discourse in the press is far more open and active (even if the reporting is not always accurate!). All across the continent, but especially in the democracies, new media outlets have emerged, exposing corruption, demanding results, keeping officials accountable for their actions, and opening the space for greater political discourse and dissent.

3. **There has been significant growth in a wide range of civil society groups, nongovernmental organizations, "watchdog" groups, and other voices aimed at monitoring government actions and improving transparency and accountability.**

As Stanford University political scientist Larry Diamond points out, a combination of older civil society organizations in Africa that date back to the colonial and immediate postcolonial periods—including student associations, trade unions, and religious bodies—and newer groups working explicitly for good governance and democracy such as think tanks, bar associations, human rights groups, women's groups, civic education groups, and election monitoring organizations, are helping to keep governments accountable:

> To a degree far beyond the early years of nationhood, the construction of democracy in Africa is a bottom-up phenomenon. Nongovernmental organizations are teaching people their rights and obligations as citizens, giving them the skills and confidence to demand accountability from their rulers, to expose and challenge corruption, to resolve conflicts peacefully, to pro-

---

19 Swarns and Onishi, "Africa Creeps Along."

mote accommodation among ethnic and religious groups, to monitor government budgets and spending, to promote community development, and to recruit and train new political leaders. Civic groups are also working at the national level to monitor elections, government budgets, and parliamentary deliberations; to expose waste, fraud, and abuses of power; and to lobby for legal reforms and institutional innovations to control corruption and improve the quality and transparency of governance." [20]

The change toward deeper democracy, increased accountability, and greater legitimacy in Africa since 1990 is unmistakable. But the changes are far from perfect, and they are far from complete. Just as it is critical to battle the pervasive pessimism and negativism that typically are used to characterize Africa, it is equally important not to be overly sanguine about Africa's dramatic political changes. These changes are a very promising beginning. But they are still new, and still fragile. It takes decades to build the institutions, public attitudes, expectations, checks on power, and other systems required for democracy to become firmly established. It took more than a century for democracy to solidify in Western Europe, and the process continues to unfold in Eastern Europe today. It took the United States 185 years to achieve universal suffrage, with numerous violent conflicts, a very bloody civil war, disputed elections, and abuses of basic human rights along the way. The process is neither fast nor easy.

Nor are there any guarantees of ultimate success. If history is any guide, it is likely that some countries unfortunately will reverse course and return to autocratic rule. Other countries may oscillate for many years, at times moving more toward democratic rule and openness only to lurch back toward more controlled systems, perhaps followed by some reopening, never quite reaching full democracy nor returning to autocratic rule. Democratization is rarely a linear and orderly process.[21]

In fact, several countries in SSA once considered democracies have shifted back into nondemocratic rule. The Gambia, one of Africa's three democracies in 1989, took a huge step backward in 1994 when Lieutenant Yahya Jammeh launched a coup and overthrew democratically elected President Dawda Jawara. The Central African Republic, the Republic of Congo, Comoros, and Guinea-Bissau all took initial steps toward democracy only to slip back later (more recently, Comoros and Guinea-Bissau have again met the threshold for democracy, but remain tenuous).

One of the most tragic situations in recent years occurred in Kenya, which had shown great promise following the election of 2002 in

---

20 Larry Diamond, *The Spirit of Democracy: The Struggle to Build Free Societies Throughout the World* (New York: Times Books, 2008), 256.

21 Thomas Carothers, "The End of the Transition Paradigm," *Journal of Democracy* 13(1): 5–21.

which Daniel arap Moi was persuaded not to run and peacefully stepped aside after 24 years as president. But the violence following Kenya's next election in late 2007 was a sobering reminder of the difficulty of establishing strong democratic norms, institutions, integrity, and a sense of fairness. Kenya followed a pattern that has been repeated throughout history all too often, including by many of the Western countries along their long path of democratization. And, of course, there continue to be difficulties in many African countries that do not meet the basic standards of democracy, including most recently Zimbabwe's marred elections.

The good news is that Kenya's and Zimbabwe's experiences are less the norm than they once would have been. Other elections in 2007, 2008, and 2009 went more smoothly, and as is usually the case when things go well, they received much less press coverage and international attention, and therefore had less influence on public perceptions.

Consider Zambia, which entered a new period of enormous political uncertainty following the death of President Levy Mwanawasa in August 2008. A close election followed on October 30, 2008, in which Rupiah Banda of Mwanawasa's MMD party won 40 percent of the vote over Michael Sata (38 percent), and Banda was sworn in on the same day. Although Sata claimed fraud and there were some demonstrations and unrest, independent monitors found the election to be generally free and fair, and overall the transition went much more smoothly than might have been the case.

Or Ghana, which showed great democratic maturity during its elections of 2008–09. President John Kufuor stepped down after eight years, and John Atta Mills defeated Nana Akufo Addo by the narrowest of margins: 50.2 percent to 49.8 percent. Voter turnout for the second round on January 2, 2009, was 73 percent (easily besting 61 percent turnout in the 2008 U.S. presidential election). While the results were close, there was no violence and there was a peaceful and successful transfer of power to an opposition party.

While in some African countries democracy remains tenuous, in others—in fact in the majority—it has continued to solidify. Of the 17 SSA countries that became democracies between 1990 and 1995, 16 are democracies today. Fourteen SSA countries consistently have met the standards for democracy for at least 13 consecutive years. Each has held multiple elections and has had at least one peaceful leadership transition through the ballot box, an occurrence almost unheard of before 1990. In other words, *the countries that began shifting toward democracy in the early 1990s are far more likely to have stuck with it and deepened democracy than reversed course.*

Africa's democracies are not perfect, and it is easy to find weaknesses. But, as Van de Walle puts it, imperfections should not diminish recent improvements:

> The gloomy view tempts us to hold African democracies to impossibly strict standards of liberal democracy, standards that even mature Western democracies cannot meet consistently. . . . Obvious imperfections should not blind us to the clear improvement in competition and participation that the 1990s have brought. We must not forget that even if day-to-day politics fall short of democratic ideals, the typical SSA country is measurably more democratic today than it was in the late 1980s.[22]

Democracy in the Emerging Countries

The discussion so far has been about the shift to democracy across SSA as a whole. What about in the 17 emerging countries? It turns out that the shift to democracy in these countries has been even more pronounced than for the continent as a whole. Thirteen of the 17 emerging countries meet the basic Freedom House and Polity IV standards to be considered democracies, and the other four have shown important shifts in that direction.[23] In addition, all six of the threshold countries meet the basic democracy standards. In most countries, the shift toward democracy and basic freedoms since the early 1990s has been quite dramatic. This change is critical for the future of the emerging countries, as it provides a cornerstone for continued growth and development.

Let's look more closely at the changes in the Freedom House and Polity IV scores for the emerging countries. The scores have improved substantially since 1989. The average Freedom House civil liberties score (scale 1 to 7, with 1 the best score) has improved from 4.9 to 2.8 over 20 years, while the improvement in the political rights score has been even larger, from 5.4 to 2.9 (Figure 3.3 shows the average of these two scores). At the same time, the average Polity IV score (scale –10 to 10, with 10 the best score) has improved from –3.9 to 4.6, a huge change.

Every one of the emerging countries has improved its Freedom House scores since 1989, with the single exception of Botswana, which already had an excellent score (Table 3.2). The same is true for all six threshold countries. In most cases the improvement has been quite large. For example, Mozambique has improved from 6.5 to 3.0, and Cape Verde has moved from 5.5 to 1.0. In only three countries have the gains been relatively small: Ethiopia, Rwanda, and Uganda. A similar pattern is evident in the Polity IV scores, with clear improvement in measures of democratic institutions in almost every one of the 17 countries.

---

22 Nicolas van de Walle, "Africa's Range of Regimes," *Journal of Democracy* 13: 66–80.

FIGURE 3.3 Political Rights and Civil Liberties Are Rising . . .

Freedom House Scores: Average of Political Rights and Civil Liberties Scores

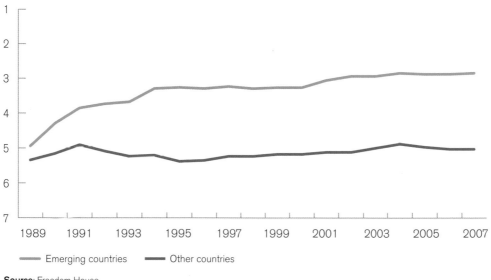

FIGURE 3.4 . . . And Democratic Institutions Are Gaining Strength

Polity IV Scores

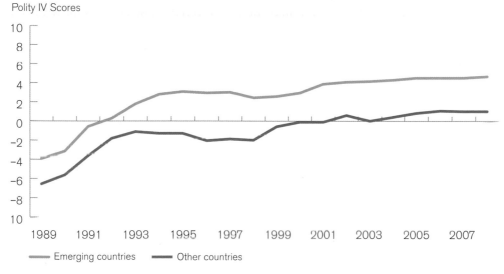

From Democracy to Governance

Beyond these basic indicators, a critical question is whether the shift to *democracy* has corresponded with improved *governance* in a broader sense, including in areas such as reduction in conflict, adherence to the rule of law, less corruption, and more effective government institutions. This is a central question for the sustainability of the emerging countries' progress into the future. It could easily be the case that countries achieve basic democratic standards without actually improving the quality of governance, or that countries improve their governance without necessarily moving toward democracy. But neither has been the case: overall in the 17 emerging countries, measureable improvements in governance have gone hand in hand with the shift toward democracy.

To begin with, there has been a significant reduction in political violence. The 1970s and 1980s were periods of intense violence across SSA, with cross-border and civil wars, assassinations, and riots affecting nearly every country across the region. As the economic crisis deepened, the Cold War came to an end, and apartheid began to collapse, political violence briefly surged in the early 1990s alongside intense political uncertainty.

But as the transition to democracy took root, incidents of political violence fell sharply, especially in the emerging countries. The most comprehensive database on political violence has been put together by Professor Arthur Banks of the State University of New York (Binghamton). Banks includes a broad range of different types of violence, including assassinations, general strikes, guerrilla warfare, government crises, purges, riots, revolutions, and antigovernment demonstrations. Looking at all of these different types of violence, between 1980 and 1995 the emerging countries saw an average of 26 violent incidents every year. But after 1996, the number of incidents dropped to an average of five per year (Figure 3.5). Political violence also declined in oil exporters and other SSA countries, but not nearly as sharply.

Turning to other dimensions of governance, let's look at the World Bank Institute's Worldwide Governance Indicators, perhaps the most widely used data measuring the quality of governance. They include six broad indicators of governance: political stability and nonviolence, rule of law, voice and accountability, government effectiveness, regulatory quality, and control of corruption. The data go back to 1996, far enough to see changes over a period that roughly coincides with the improved growth rates of the emerging economies.

For SSA as a whole, the indicators show no overall change in the average quality of governance since 1996. But the lack of change in the aggre-

TABLE 3.2 The Shift to Democracy in the Emerging Countries

Freedom House and Polity IV Scores

	Freedom House 7 = worst score 1 = best score		Polity IV Score −10 = worst score +10 = best score	
Emerging Countries	**1989**	**2008**	**1989**	**2008**
Botswana	1.5	2	7	8
Burkina Faso	5.5	4	−7	0
Cape Verde	5.5	1	N/A	N/A
Ethiopia	7	5	−8	1
Ghana	5.5	1.5	−7	8
Lesotho	5.5	2.5	−7	8
Mali	6	2.5	−7	6
Mauritius	2	1.5	10	10
Mozambique	6.5	3	−7	6
Namibia	3.5	2	6*	6
Rwanda	6	5.5	−7	−3
São Tomé and Príncipe	5.5	2	N/A	N/A
Seychelles	6	3	N/A	N/A
South Africa	5.5	2	4	9
Tanzania	6	3.5	−6	−1
Uganda	5	4.5	−7	−1
Zambia	5.5	3	−9	7
Threshold Countries				
Benin	7	2	−7	7
Kenya	6	3.5	−6	6
Liberia	5.5	3.5	−6	6
Malawi	6.5	4	−9	6
Senegal	3.5	3	−1	8
Sierra Leone	5.5	3	−7	7

* Namibia's Polity IV score in 1989 is not available, but subsequent scores rate it consistently with a 6.
Source: Freedom House and Polity IV.

FIGURE 3.5 Political Conflict Has Fallen Sharply in the Emerging Countries

Average Number of Domestic Conflict Incidents per Year

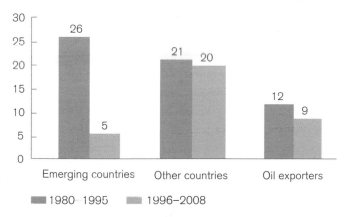

Source: Cross-National Time-Series Data Archive, www.databanksinternational.com.

gate disguises two opposing trends: *on each governance indicator, the emerging countries have shown clear improvement on average, while other countries in the region have registered clear deterioration* (Figure 3.6).

For example, on control of corruption, the average score for the emerging countries has improved from –0.28 to –0.05 (the global scores range from about –2.5 to +2.5, with 0.0 the global median). The average country ranking has improved from 104nd to 89th between 1996 and 2008. But at the same time, for other countries in SSA, the average control of corruption score worsened from –0.57 to –0.92 and the average country ranking fell from 140th to 148th. A similar pattern is evident in the other five governance indicators. Notably on two of the indicators—"voice and accountability" and "political stability"—the emerging countries' score is now higher than the worldwide median.

Thus, since the mid-1990s Africa's emerging countries have seen accelerated economic growth, a shift toward democracy, and improvements in governance. What is the relationship among the three? It appears that they are connected in a virtuous circle in which improvements in one area help support improvements in the others. In most cases, the Freedom House and Polity IV scores began to improve first, but the acceleration in economic growth and improvement in governance began very soon thereafter. It is probably the case that the strengthening of democracy helped improve the quality of governance, but improvements in the quality of governance almost certainly have helped sustain democracy. Similarly, the improvements in democracy and governance have helped put into place better economic policies that have helped accelerate growth, while the faster growth rates have helped deliver tangible benefits to citizens that reinforce the shift to democracy and better governance. While dictatorship, poor governance, and weak economic performance created a self-reinforcing negative cycle during the late 1970s and 1980s, since the mid-1990s democracy, stronger governance, and improved economic performance have created a positive self-reinforcing cycle, with each supporting improvements in the others.

But what really matters is the future. In the emerging countries there has been a fundamental shift in the quality of leadership, away from the days when dictators used national resources as their personal assets and toward governments that actually serve and are accountable to their citizens. These changes bode well for Africa's emerging economies. The shift toward more democratic, accountable, and legitimate governments with improved governance provides a strong foundation to sustain and accelerate the progress they have achieved since the mid-1990s. Other changes under way should help reinforce this trend, as we will see in the chapters that follow.

FIGURE 3.6 Governance Is Improving in Emerging Africa, but Worsening Elsewhere

Worldwide Governance Indicators (a score of zero is the median for all countries in the world)

Rule of Law

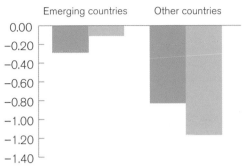

Regulatory Quality

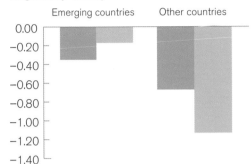

Government Effectiveness

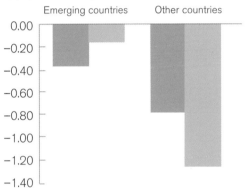

Control of Corruption

Voice and Accountability

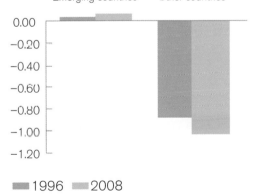

Political Stability

◼◼◼ 1996   ◼◼◼ 2008

Source: World Bank Institute, Worldwide Governance Indicators 1996–2008, accessed July 2009.

BOX 3.1

Defining Democracy

Deciding which countries are democracies is far from straightforward: there is no universally accepted definition. No single institution or event constitutes democracy. Competitive elections are a key component, but elections alone cannot guarantee true democracy. It is a process rather than an event. It has many facets, including popular sovereignty through either majority rule or representation; freedom of speech and the press; the rule of law; protection of minority rights, civil liberties and basic human rights; civilian control over the military; and systems for accountability and checks on power.

There are, however, several internationally recognized indices and rankings of democracies. Two of the most widely used are Freedom House's *Freedom in the World* index and the University of Maryland/George Mason University *Polity IV Index of Political Regime*

Characteristics and Transitions. The two indices capture different but complementary characteristics usually associated with democracy. Both are used here to categorize countries as democracies.

Freedom House is primarily a *rights-based* index that provides a comparative assessment of the extent to which political rights and civil liberties are honored. The Freedom House index does not explicitly measure democracy, but rather focuses on the basic rights and freedoms that are generally seen as integral to democracy. Based on a checklist of 25 questions, the index gives 193 countries and territories around the world a score from 1 (the highest level of freedom) to 7 (the lowest level) on two separate indices of political rights and civil liberties. The two scores are averaged to determine an overall "freedom status" for each country. Freedom House considers countries and territories with a combined average score of 2.5 or below to be "free," those with scores between 3 and 5 to be "partly free," and those with scores of 5.5 or above to be "not free." Those in the "free" category are generally considered to be democracies, along with some in the "partly free" group. For our purposes, a country must be in the top half of the Freedom House rankings with a combined score of 4 or below to be considered a democracy.

The Polity IV index focuses primarily on *institutions*. It is based less on judgment than on measurable characteristics of regime type and political authority. The polity index measures the competitiveness and openness of elections, constraints on executive power, regulations on political expression, the duration of regime type, and other institutional measures of authority and governance. Thus, Polity IV focuses on measuring the authority that the government wields, whereas Freedom House aims to measure the freedoms that the government protects.

The hallmark composite Polity variable is a 21-point measure ranging from –10 (most autocratic) to +10 (most democratic). Most analysts consider countries with a score greater than zero to be democracies, and that is the standard that we use.

Countries that achieve both standards (a Freedom House score of 4 or below and a Polity IV score of 0 or above) are considered democracies in this book. (Polity IV does not have scores for Cape Verde, São Tomé and Príncipe, or the Seychelles, but because of their strong Freedom House scores, they count as democracies here). The two indices generally are consistent with each other, as would be expected. Greater political freedoms and stronger political institutions typically go hand in hand. Seven countries meet one standard but not the other in the latest Freedom House (2008) and Polity IV (2008) scores: Djibouti, Burundi, the Democratic Republic of the Congo, Tanzania, Nigeria, Côte d'Ivoire, and Ethiopia. Using the combined standard, only three countries in sub-Saharan Africa were democracies in 1989; by 2008 the number had grown to 23.

STRONGER
ECONOMIC
MANAGEMENT

By 1983, Ghana's economy had hit rock bottom. The hope that followed Kwame Nkrumah's declaration of independence in 1957 had long since evaporated. The 1966 coup d'état that overthrew Nkrumah had touched off 15 years of intense political instability and a series of coups and countercoups that led to eight different heads of state holding power between 1966 and 1981. The combination of sharply rising oil prices, falling cocoa prices, extreme political volatility, and poor economic management in the late 1970s left the country in disarray. As global economic shocks roiled the economy, successive governments responded with heavy intervention, making a bad situation worse. They imposed extensive trade restrictions, fixed the exchange rate at artificially low levels, and introduced stringent price controls, including imposing very low prices on cocoa farmers. They rapidly expanded the civil service from 35,000 in 1972 to 300,000 in 1982. The government took full or partial ownership of more than 200 enterprises, about half of the modern sector.[1]

The economy went into freefall. Government revenues collapsed just as spending expanded, falling from 21 percent of GDP in 1970 to just 5 percent of a smaller GDP in 1983. The budget deficit ballooned, so the government began to borrow heavily. And when it could no longer borrow abroad, it turned to the central bank to finance the difference, leading to explosive money creation. Inflation jumped to over 120 percent, even in the face of

Opposite:
Counting
Tanzanian shillings
in Dar es Salaam
(©2010 Mikkel
Ostergaard / Panos)

---

1 James Brooke, "Ghana, Once Hopeless, Gets At Least the Look of Success," *New York Times,* January 3, 1989, http://www.nytimes.com/1989/01/03/world/ghana-once-hopeless-gets-at-least-the-look-of-success.html.

widespread price controls. At the same time, foreign exchange reserves dried up, and as dollars disappeared, black markets became pervasive.[2]

The result was disaster. Average income fell by a stunning one-third between 1970 and 1983. Poverty soared. New investment all but disappeared. Cocoa exports fell by half, as did production of staple crops. As Ghana's economy collapsed and neighboring oil-rich Nigeria boomed in the 1970s, people voted with their feet, and more than 2 million Ghanaians fled for Nigeria, only to be expelled and forced back in January 1983. Drought and bush fires pushed the country to the brink of disaster. Ghana's early promise had gone badly wrong.

In April 1983, the government of President Jerry Rawlings decided to act. It introduced the wide-ranging Economy Recovery Program in an attempt to get the economy back on track. Its initial focus was government finances. It began to cut expenditures and strengthen tax collection, bringing the budget deficit from over 6 percent of GDP in 1982 to near zero by 1986. With the smaller deficit, the government stopped printing money, bringing about a sharp fall in inflation. It introduced a series of devaluations and removed many trade restrictions, boosting export activity. When it introduced foreign exchange bureaus in 1998, the currency market stabilized and black markets for dollars essentially disappeared. It raised producer prices for cocoa, and with the fall in inflation, the real price of cocoa paid to farmers tripled by the late 1980s, reversing a decade of decline. The government removed a wide range of price controls, and while prices initially rose, they soon stabilized as goods came back on the market and shortages disappeared. Later, the government began to privatize many state-owned enterprises, further helping its finances and strengthening the management of these companies.

The result has been a striking turnaround. The Ghanaian economy today bears little resemblance to the basket case of the early 1980s. Economic growth has averaged 5 percent per year for 25 years, translating into a 70 percent increase in the income of the average Ghanaian. The poverty rate, after dropping only slightly from 53 percent in 1984 to 50 percent in 1993 in the early days of the reform program, fell dramatically to 30 percent by 2005. Life expectancy was 53 years in 1980; today it is 60 years. The private sector, after waiting for several years for the reforms to solidify, has responded enthusiastically. Investment, which had dropped to just 7 percent of GDP between 1978 and 1984, has risen to more than 25 percent of a much larger GDP, and exports have risen to 37 percent of GDP. The economy is more diversified, with the over-reliance on cocoa

---

2 Ernest Aryeetey and Augustin Fosu, "Economic Growth in Ghana, 1960–2000," in *The Political Economy of Economic Growth in Africa, 1960–2000,* Volume 2, ed. Ndulu, et al. (Cambridge: Cambridge University Press, 2008).

supplanted by larger contributions from minerals, timber, manufacturing, and a growing range of nontraditional exports, including furniture, pineapples, tuna, and data entry services.

In the late 1990s, as the economy began to stabilize and then expand, Ghana began to shift from authoritarian rule to democracy. It substantially strengthened political rights, civil liberties, and basic freedoms, and its indictors of governance have improved markedly. It held peaceful and competitive elections in 2000, 2004, and 2008. Remarkably, in both 2000 and 2008, opposition candidates won the contest with smooth and peaceful transitions of power, an unthinkable outcome just 20 years before. "In Ghana, we know how to have a democracy," said Doris Quartey, a teacher who was preparing to vote in the 2008 presidential runoff election. "We are an example for the whole continent."[3]

Ghana's record is far from spotless. The progress over the last 20 years at times has been uneven, and there are still many flaws. Nevertheless, overall progress has been strong, and the major changes in economic policy and governance provide a strong foundation for continued growth in the future.

※ ※ ※

Ghana's story of economic malaise and self-inflicted wounds was repeated across much of sub-Saharan Africa in the 1970s and 1980s. The problems were not all the result of poor policies and governance; SSA clearly was dealt a bad hand through the corrosive effects of colonialism, poor geography, endemic disease, and the global economic turmoil of the 1970s, all of which made the development challenge in Africa far more difficult than in many other places. But all the same, there is no doubt that economic mismanagement made the situation much worse.[4]

Yet just as poor economic management generated dismal economic performance through the 1980s, major improvements in economic policymaking played a central role in the economic turnaround in the mid-1990s, especially in the emerging countries. And improved economic policies are a cornerstone for continuing economic progress into the future.

SSA's economic deterioration began in the mid-1970s, when many governments responded to the global economic crisis by sharply increasing spending and budget deficits, and then financing the deficits either by borrowing abroad or printing money at home. The first led to a rapid build-up in foreign debt, the second to growing inflation. Most countries

---

3 Lydia Polgreen, "Ghana's Image, Glowing Abroad, Is Beginning to Show a Few Blemishes at Home," *New York Times*, December 22, 2008, http://www.nytimes.com/2008/12/23/world/africa/23ghana.html.

4 For the most comprehensive analysis of economic performance in SSA since 1960, see Benno Ndulu, et al., *The Political Economy of Economic Growth in Africa, 1960–2000*, vols. 1 and 2 (Cambridge: Cambridge University Press, 2007).

fixed their exchange rates at overvalued rates to try to keep import prices low for their favored political constituencies—typically urban consumers, the army, and the civil service. But this approach only encouraged rapid growth in imports while undermining the profitability of exporters and domestic firms competing with imports.

As imports grew, governments introduced ad hoc trade barriers to try to stop them. They gave favored firms generous protection through high import tariffs and quotas. While sometimes well-designed import substitution policies can help stimulate domestic industries, more often than not these policies were abused as tools of political patronage to protect industries that could never hope to be competitive. In some countries, exports were heavily taxed or restricted to divert supplies to domestic markets and keep prices artificially low. The result of all these policies was to kill new business creation, limit economic diversification, undermine job creation, and generate big trade deficits. Only poverty flourished.

As trade deficits grew, foreign exchange became scarce. Central bank holdings of foreign exchange were cut in half, from the equivalent of 15 weeks of import cover on average in 1973 to less than 8 weeks in 1982. As the availability of hard currency dwindled, black markets emerged, and the exchange rate in those markets soared. In the early 1980s, the average black market premium on foreign exchange reached 60 percent, and in some countries it was much worse. In Ghana, the black market premium reached an astonishing 40 times the official rate in 1982, and in Mozambique it was nearly 50 times higher in 1986. The shortages of currency severely distorted markets throughout the economy and set up easy opportunities for corruption. Government officials could obtain scarce foreign exchange at the official (cheap) rate for their friends and cronies, of course accompanied by an easy bribe. Those without connections were left to buy dollars on the street at a much higher rate.

Meanwhile, farmers struggled mightily. The "urban bias" against agriculture started with overvalued exchange rates that kept food prices cheap and undermined agricultural exports. It was worsened by government price controls, limited access to seeds and fertilizers, poor roads, and weak agricultural extension and research programs. Among the most damaging approaches, as documented in Robert Bates' brilliant 1981 work *Markets and States in Tropical Africa,* were pervasive agriculture marketing boards. These institutions ostensibly were established to provide farmers with a sure market to sell their goods, but in reality they were run primarily to control the market, drive down prices, and transfer the surplus to government (and often personal) coffers.[5]

---

5   Robert Bates, *Markets and States in Tropical Africa: The Political Basis of Agricultural Policies,* (Berkeley: University of California Press, 1981).

In most countries, the state intervened in the economy with a heavy hand. State enterprises controlled grocery stores, trading houses, plantations, banks, utilities, hotels, and manufacturing companies. Government regulations added layers of bureaucracy that stifled business and encouraged graft. The balance between government involvement and private enterprise was way off kilter, and the heavy involvement of the state did significant economic damage.

Sometimes bad policies were just mistakes by inexperienced policymakers struggling in the face of global economic turmoil. After all, economic management was extremely complicated in the global environment of the late 1970s and early 1980s –almost every country in the world went into a deep recession—and skilled technocrats were in short supply across Africa. Sometimes policies were based on well-intentioned ideas and ideologies, with many African leaders experimenting with various forms of socialism, often encouraged by foreign advisors and academics. But often they were driven by government leaders who were unaccountable to their people and far more interested in enlarging their economic and political power, supporting their cronies, and funneling money to their personal bank accounts rather than in creating opportunities to encourage development and poverty reduction. As I have stressed, political authoritarianism and heavy-handed economic policy controls went hand in hand across SSA.

Kampala, Uganda

Whatever the reason for the policy choices, the effects were devastating. Economies across the continent stagnated and in some cases collapsed entirely. The median income fell by about 15 percent in SSA between 1977 and 1995, and average poverty rates rose to 59 percent. In some cases it was much worse. By the mid-1980s Africa's tragedy was in full swing.

The most comprehensive and authoritative assessment of Africa's economic performance during this period is the *Economic Growth in Africa* research project undertaken by a team at the Africa Economic Research Consortium (AERC).[6] Based on an exhaustive multiyear analysis that examined countries across the continent, the team identified and carefully catalogued four key "antigrowth syndromes" that it found were at the root of Africa's poor growth performance:

- Aggressive *control or regulatory policy regimes* in which governments displaced the market as the primary agency for governing the economy, resulting in severe distortions of economic activity and rewards for corruption;

- *Ethno-regional redistribution systems* that compromised efficiency and economic growth by redistributing substantial amounts of income to specific political interest groups, often along ethnic or regional lines;

- *Intertemporal redistribution policies* that aggressively sacrificed the future income of subsequent generations for present gain through high levels of unsustainable spending, the accumulation of massive debts, and looting of publicly owned assets; and

- *State breakdown* during civil war or periods of intense political instability.

Almost all SSA countries experienced one, and in most cases more than one, of these syndromes for prolonged periods before the mid-1990s. The only sustained exceptions were, not surprisingly, Botswana and Mauritius. Otherwise, the syndromes were pervasive: in the 1960s about 50 percent of Africans were living in a country with at least one syndrome, whereas in the 1970s it jumped to 89 percent and in the 1980s soared to 94 percent. Nearly the entire subcontinent was inhospitable to growth. The researchers found that these syndromes were a key driver of Africa's dismal economic performance and argued that their removal would be central to any economic turnaround. They concluded that remaining syndrome-free is the single most important choice for closing the growth gap between Africa and other regions.

---

6 Ndulu, et al., *Political Economy.*

The Turnaround in Economic Policies

Today the situation in SSA is very different. Governments across Africa have made major changes in economic policies, especially (but not only) in the emerging countries. Gone are the days of hyperinflation, multiple exchange rates, and black markets to buy foreign currency. Budget management is much more prudent, with smaller deficits, more publicly disclosed audits, much less borrowing against future generations, and lower rates of inflation. Marketing boards have largely disappeared, and trade policies are less restrictive and arbitrary. The state still plays an active role in most countries, but the extreme versions of the heavy hand of the state that were prevalent across the continent have given way to a better balance between states and markets.

Ghana was one of the first to introduce widespread policy changes with its 1983 Economic Reform Program. By the late 1980s, many other countries had at least begun the process.

Three main forces were behind the changes: the lack of available financing for continuing the old patterns, changing ideas, and global pressures. As budget and trade deficits began to grow in the late 1970s, countries across SSA financed them by some combination of borrowing abroad or at home, printing money, and running down foreign exchange reserves. But there was only so long they could continue on this path. Once Mexico defaulted on its debts in 1982, foreign banks stopped lending to developing countries worldwide, and foreign borrowing options disappeared. The amounts available to borrow at home were limited, and most countries quickly exhausted their foreign exchange reserves. With financing options drying up, governments had little choice but to introduce painful austerity measures to close their deficits, usually under the auspices of the International Monetary Fund. As discussed in the last chapter, these austerity measures were enormously unpopular, and contributed significantly to the rise of political protests in the late 1980s. But governments had little choice; they were out of room to maneuver.

As much as governments were forced to introduce these measures, changing ideas played an important role as well. It became obvious to economists, business leaders, and the general public that the economic policies and heavy state control of the past had failed. A growing number of policymakers, academics, and other leaders learned from the mistakes of the past and came to recognize that governments could not impose absolute controls over prices and commerce, and that doing so led to capital flight, corruption, debt, stagnation, and poverty. A different approach was required.

The policy changes initially focused on painful but necessary macroeconomic stabilization, especially reducing budget deficits, devaluing currencies, removing price controls, and reigning in inflation. Over the years they expanded to include privatization and other state-owned enterprise reforms, strengthening of agricultural price policies, lowering of tariffs and other trade barriers, easing of regulations and controls on businesses, and a wide range of other changes.

At first, economies stabilized but did not begin to grow. Budget deficits shrank, inflation began to fall, black markets disappeared, and shortages became less frequent. But overall economic output and income remained stagnant. It took several years for the policy changes to begin to affect investment and output, to a large extent because of the dramatic political changes that occurred between 1989 and 1994, as described in the previous chapter. With so much political uncertainty, investors remained cautious, capital flight remained high, and output remained flat. But as the political situation began to stabilize, the combination of new, more accountable governments and improved economic policies began to take hold. By 1995, a new period of economic expansion had begun.

The extent of the change in economic policies in the emerging countries is succinctly captured by changes in the prevalence of the four "antigrowth syndromes" described earlier (Figure 4.1). In the 1970s, antigrowth syndromes were on the rise across SSA, and remained high for more than a decade. But beginning in the mid-1980s, and especially in the late 1980s and early 1990s, they fell sharply in the emerging countries. By comparison, they fell only gradually in the oil-exporting countries and hardly at all in the other countries of SSA. By 1995, the emerging countries were essentially syndrome-free, setting the stage for the turnaround in economic growth.

Broadly speaking, the shift in economic policies has been a move away from heavy state intervention and toward fairly orthodox economic policies. While the move toward more market-oriented policies was often criticized at the time (and still is), in retrospect it is clear that this shift paid off with much better economic performance. That is not to say that pure free markets or strong orthodoxy are always right. They aren't. There is a role for governments to play in making markets work more effectively, especially in implementing appropriate regulations, establishing strong legal frameworks, and providing vital services. But the balance between markets and states was way off in SSA in the early 1980s, and the shift in policies during the last two decades has brought about a much healthier and effective balance. Looking back it is clear that the shift from statist control toward more market-oriented policies has had a big payoff.

Of course, economic management is far from perfect despite significant improvement since the late 1980s. Being syndrome-free does not

FIGURE 4.1 The Emerging Countries Eliminated Many of the Major Barriers to Growth in the Early 1990s

Number of Antigrowth Syndromes

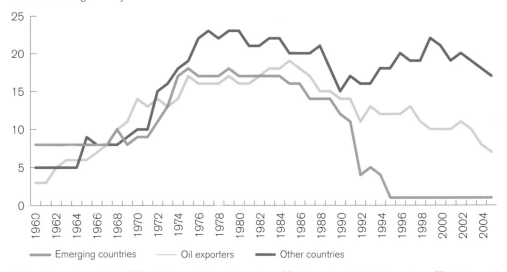

Antigrowth syndromes include (1) control or regulatory policy regimes, (2) ethno-regional distributions systems, (3) intertemporal redistribution policies, and (4) state breakdown, as defined and catalogued in Benno Ndulu, et al., *The Political Economy of Economic Growth in Africa, 1960-2000*, vols. 1 and 2 (Cambridge: Cambridge University Press, 2008).

mean that economic policies are ideal. It is still easy to find counterproductive regulations, arduous red tape, price controls, and business restrictions that ultimately support only political friends (which, to some extent, can be found in every country in the world). But the difference today compared to 20 years ago is unmistakable, especially in the emerging countries. And the policy changes that helped spark the turnaround in the mid-1990s have been deepened and strengthened over time, helping to lay the foundation for continued growth into the future.

Exchange Rate, Trade, and Budget Policies

Let's take a closer look at some of the key policy changes, starting with exchange rates. Since the late 1980s many countries have moved to flexible exchange rates and as a result have essentially eliminated overvaluation. Where exchange rates remain fixed (such as in the West African and Central African Monetary Unions), they are pegged at more competitive rates. The once ubiquitous black markets for foreign currency are gone in the emerging countries. Multiple exchange rates have disappeared, and with them the shortages of foreign exchange.

Figure 4.2 shows one indicator of the decline in overvaluation: the "real" exchange rate, which incorporates changes in the nominal exchange rate alongside relative inflation at home and abroad.[7] African currencies were massively overvalued in the early 1980s, but they have gradually depreciated in real terms since then, through both depreciation of the nominal exchange rate and better control of inflation. Today, most countries are at or near parity.

This change has made a huge difference. In Uganda, for example, massive exchange rate overvaluation in the late 1970s and early 1980s severely undermined investment and destroyed export profitability. The black market premium reached 100 percent in the mid-1980s. Beginning in the late 1980s, the government first devalued the shilling, and then liberalized the foreign exchange market system and introduced foreign exchange bureaus. The spread between the official and parallel rates all but disappeared. Alongside a package of other trade, price, and monetary reforms, the economy responded. Investment grew from 11 percent of GDP in 1989 to 20 percent in 1996. Exports expanded quickly, with diversification into horticulture and other new products. Foreign exchange reserves increased substantially, from US$44 million in 1990 to over US$800 million a decade later.

FIGURE 4.2 Currencies Are Much Less Overvalued Today than in the 1980s
Change in the Real Exchange Rate

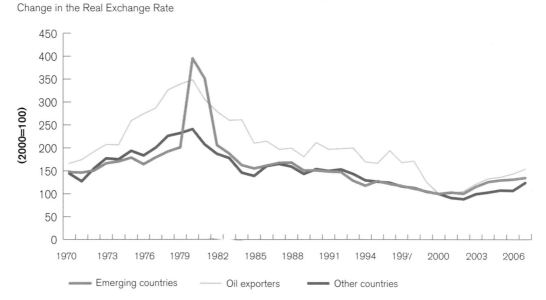

Note: Excludes Ghana, Sudan, and Zimbabwe, where exchange rates were extremely overvalued.
Source: Author's calculations (see footnote 7).

---

7 The real exchange rate is estimated here by the common method of multiplying the nominal exchange rate (in foreign units of currency per unit of local currency) times the ratio of the domestic consumer price index relative to the U.S. consumer price index.

As currency markets have stabilized and black markets have disappeared, shortages of foreign exchange have become rare, and holdings of foreign exchange reserves have grown. In the emerging countries, foreign exchange reserves have doubled from about two months of import cover in the late 1980s to over four months in 2007 (Figure 4.3). In several countries, including Botswana, Rwanda, São Tomé and Príncipe, Tanzania, and Uganda, reserve cover now exceeds five months of imports. The growth in reserves has helped stabilize currency fluctuations, helped reduce investment risk, and created a buffer to cushion the impact of the 2009 global financial crisis.

Meanwhile, trade policies are much more open. In the early 1980s, tariff rates across SSA averaged over 25 percent. Today they have been cut in half, to an average of less than 12 percent in the emerging countries, similar to other developing regions around the world. In the other countries in Africa, tariffs have dropped to around 15 percent (Figure 4.4). Quantitative restrictions on imports and taxes on exports have declined significantly. As a result, businesses can import much more easily and cheaply, and competitive firms are beginning to either displace imports or export to world markets. Partly because of these changes, trade has expanded rapidly in the emerging countries, as we showed earlier in Chapter 2.

FIGURE 4.3 Foreign Exchange Reserves Are Rising

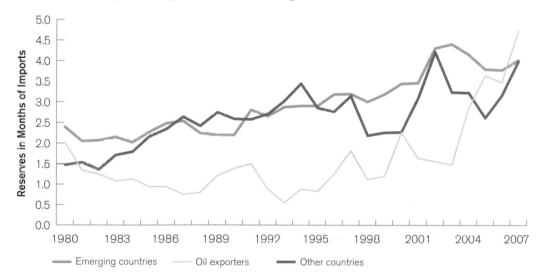

Source: World Bank, World Development Indictors. Data for emerging countries exclude Botswana, whose reserves are very large.

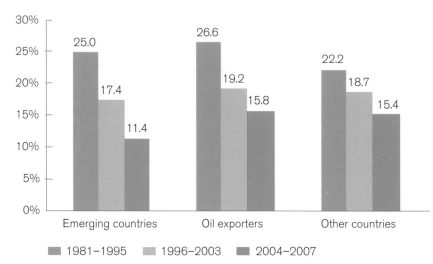

FIGURE 4.4 Import Tariff Rates Have Fallen Steadily
Average Import Tariff Rate

Source: World Bank data on trade and import barriers, http://go.worldbank.org/LGOXFTV550.

Improved Incentives for Agriculture

Among the most important policy changes have been those in agriculture. The once strong urban bias that undermined farmer incentives has shifted considerably. Governments once imposed controls to keep prices low for consumers at the expense of farmers; today, the worst of those controls have been removed, and farmers can sell their products for much better prices. Agricultural marketing boards that had nearly exclusive power to buy farm products at depressed prices have given way to more open and competitive markets where farmers can choose from a variety of options to sell their goods for the best possible price. Taxes on agricultural production are much lower, especially for export products.

One way to see the reduction in the bias against agriculture is the change in the so-called nominal rate of assistance, a composite measure of the impact of policies on incentives for farm production compiled by the World Bank. A negative value indicates a net bias against agriculture, such as from heavy taxes, export restrictions, or government-controlled low prices. Zero indicates an overall neutral policy stance, and a positive number indicates a net bias in favor of agriculture, such as through subsidies or import protection.

In 1988, the net bias against agriculture in the emerging countries was more than 17 percent of output prices, equivalent to a huge tax that was a crippling burden for farmers (Figure 4.5). But by 2004 the bias had

FIGURE 4.5 Agricultural Policies Are Much More Favorable

The Nominal Rate of Assistance, Total Agriculture

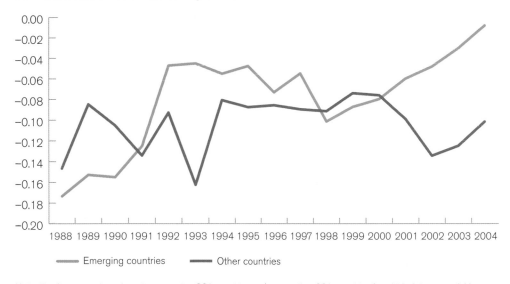

Note: The figures are based on nine emerging SSA countries and seven other SSA countries for which data are available. A negative score indicates a policy bias against agriculture, a score of zero indicates an overall neutral policy stance, and a positive score indicates an overall policy bias in favor of agriculture.

Source: World Bank Dataset on Agricultural Distortions; Kym Anderson and William A. Masters, eds., *Distortions to Agricultural Incentives in Africa* (Washington, DC: World Bank, 2009).

been nearly eliminated through deregulation of farm gate prices, lower taxes, elimination of export taxes, and reduced influence of state-owned market boards. Farmers have responded energetically. As we saw in Chapter 2, the annual rate of growth in agricultural production has averaged more than 3.5 percent for 20 years across these countries, meaning that total agricultural production has nearly doubled since 1988 in the emerging countries.

Mozambique is a good example. Following independence from Portugal in 1975, the government nationalized several agricultural firms and took over land that had been abandoned by fleeing settlers, which led to the creation of large state-owned farms. By the 1980s, these farms controlled more than 50 percent of agricultural production. In addition, the government continued the colonial practice of requiring that all commercial agricultural goods be sold through a marketing board that controlled farm prices at low levels. It was by all accounts a disaster: agricultural production fell 30 percent between 1975 and 1982.

But starting in 1987, the government allowed private traders to enter the market, sold several state-owned enterprises, and liberalized prices. Prices received by farmers rose significantly, providing much stronger incentives for farmers and raising farm income. Following the end of the civil war in 1992, the economy rebounded quickly, including the agricultural sector. The government continued to improve incentives for farmers throughout the 1990s. The nominal rate of assistance has increased dramatically, from –35 percent in the late 1970s (reflecting the very low prices imposed on farmers) to +12 percent since 2000 (reflecting the freeing of prices, alongside import protection on certain products). The combination of the end of the conflict, the strengthening of macroeconomic policies, and the improvement in incentives to farmers has led to growth in agricultural production averaging more than 6 percent per year since 1992, so that production has more than doubled since then.[8]

Strengthening the Business Climate

Beyond agriculture, the overall climate for private business has strengthened markedly across Africa in the last few years, but especially in the emerging countries. There has been a considerable decline in the costs to start a business, the extent of red tape and restrictions on business, the costs of registering property, the hassles in pursuing commercial court claims, and other difficulties of conducting business.

Consider the costs of starting a business.[9] One of the major reasons private sector growth was so slow in SSA during the 1980s and early 1990s was that it was just too expensive even to start a business. Energetic entrepreneurs with creative ideas couldn't get started because of the morass of permits, signatures, and processes they needed to wade through, not to mention the high fees (and accompanying bribes) at every step of the process.

But this has begun to change. Governments typically no longer see private business as something to be suspicious of, to control, or to extract resources from, but rather as key drivers of long-term development that should be encouraged and supported. In many countries, the barriers to start a business have been significantly reduced, making it easier for investors and entrepreneurs to get moving.

For example, many countries have introduced one-stop investment shops, making it possible for investors to get all the permits and forms they need in one place, rather than taking months to run around to different offices. Several have reduced the number of required permits and registrations, and eliminated unnecessary steps. Ghana, for example, has

---

8 Andrea Alfieri, Channing Arndt, and Xavier Cirera, "Mozambique," in *Distortions to Agricultural Incentives in Africa,* eds. Kym Anderson and William A. Masters (Washington, DC: World Bank, 2009).

9 In this section I rely heavily on the rich analyses and databases generated by the World Bank Group's *Doing Business* Project. The annual *Doing Business* reports and the online database are particularly useful, both in generating data and—by reporting comparative data across countries—in encouraging countries to accelerate the pace of reform. See http://www.doingbusiness.org.

eliminated the need to register a company seal, an unnecessary annoyance. Several countries, including Botswana, Namibia, and South Africa, have introduced faster online registration systems. Liberia, Sierra Leone, and South Africa, among others, have made the use of lawyers optional for registration, reducing both the time and costs for businesses.

The result has been a significant drop in the costs to start a business across almost all of Africa, but especially in the emerging countries (Figure 4.6). In 2003, starting a business cost the equivalent of 1.3 times average annual income per capita in the emerging countries, but just six years later the costs were only about 0.3 times average income.

Similarly, the costs of licenses and construction permits have dropped sharply in many countries. Burkina Faso has reduced the cost of construction permits by 25 percent and has cut 12 days out of the process. It introduced a one-stop shop, cut in half the fees for soil exams, and reduced fees for municipal approvals and for fire safety. It also limited the number of onsite inspections by the government, eliminating the frequent and random inspections that used to plague builders. One architect in Ougadougou reports that "we can still expect inspections at certain critical stages, but this is a far cry from the up to 15 or so we could receive before."[10]

FIGURE 4.6 The Costs of Starting a Business Have Fallen Sharply
Start-Up Costs as a Percentage of Income per Capita

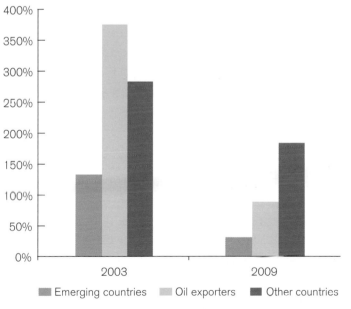

Source: World Bank *Doing Business 2010* (see n. 9).

---

10 World Bank, *Doing Business 2009.*

Other countries have followed suit. Liberia now processes building permits in 30 days, and has cut the fees from US$1,400 to US$700. Rwanda has combined the applications for location clearance and a building permit into a single form, and companies need to submit only one application form for water, sewerage, and electricity connections.[11]

It is also getting easier to register property in many countries, easing disputes about land and making it easier to collateralize loans. In 2008, Rwanda replaced an expensive registration fee costing 6 percent of the value of the property with a simple flat fee of 20,000 Rwandan francs (about US$34). In addition to the fee, the Rwandan Revenue Authority previously had to value the property, which took 35 days on average (and introduced ample opportunity for bribes). With the flat fee, the valuation requirement is no longer necessary. Registering property now requires just four procedures and costs on average less than 1 percent of the property value.

Property registration has always had a strong gender bias, since many countries allow only men to own and register property. The World Bank quotes a woman named Catherine who describes the situation in Lesotho: "The process is slow for everyone, but especially for women. I wanted to sell our store last year, but since my husband was abroad, I had to wait two months for him to return and sign. When he signed the papers for me, the deal went through—after three more months of bureaucracy." But Lesotho has now taken steps to remove this bias. A law passed in November 2006 allows married women in Lesotho to transfer property without their husbands' signatures.[12]

The overall improvement in the business climate in the emerging countries of Africa is evident in the World Bank's *Doing Business* rankings (Table 4.1). Across 10 different indicators of the business climate, the emerging countries on average rank in the upper two-thirds of countries around the world; on every indicator, they rank higher than the average for low-income countries. Out of 181 countries worldwide, the emerging countries rank on average 104, a significant improvement over previous years, and higher than the average for low-income countries around the world. In the 2009 rankings, the country with the largest improvement in the world was Rwanda, and Liberia ranked in the top 10 in improvement.

Make no mistake—business costs remain high in the emerging countries. It is still hard to get a business started in many places, and red tape and unnecessary costs add to the burden along the way. There is still a long way to go to make the business environments competitive in several countries, but change is clearly under way.

---

11 Ibid.

12 World Bank, *Doing Business 2008* (see n. 9).

TABLE 4.1 Ease of Doing Business
Average Rank out of 181 Countries Worldwide, 2009

	Sub-Saharan Africa		Low-income countries (worldwide)
	Emerging countries	Other countries	
Total Ease of Doing Business	**104**	**159**	**141**
Starting a business	100	149	118
Dealing with construction permits	101	126	124
Employing workers	97	127	114
Registering property	103	136	118
Getting credit	99	139	123
Protecting investors	85	140	115
Paying taxes	78	126	120
Trading across borders	126	136	141
Enforcing contracts	83	133	113
Closing a business	108	139	135

Source: The World Bank, *Doing Business 2010* (see n. 9).

Private investors and entrepreneurs have responded to these changes. The combination of improvements in macroeconomic policies, agricultural incentives, and the business climate has led to significant increases in investment, from both domestic entrepreneurs and foreign investors. Whereas investment in the emerging countries averaged about 18 percent of GDP in the 1980s, since 1996 it has averaged nearly 23 percent. In constant dollar terms, annual aggregate investment since 2004 has been more than *double* the level of the late 1980s. Most investment comes from domestic entrepreneurs, but a large share of the increase in recent years has come from foreign investors, who are beginning to see growing opportunities in the emerging SSA countries. Foreign direct investment averaged a paltry 0.8 percent of GDP in the emerging countries in the 1980s, but since 1996 it has averaged 4.0 percent, more than quadrupling its share of GDP.

Sustaining the Progress

The deep changes in economic policy that began in the mid-1980s have been a central part of the renaissance of the emerging countries. By the same token, continuing strong economic management and further deepening and extending the reform process will be fundamental to continuing that success in the years to come.

One reason for guarded optimism for the future is that countries today have much stronger professional and technical capacity for economic policymaking than they did 20 years ago. Central banks in particular have far more well-trained and capable policy analysts and researchers. Ministries of finance and planning, investment commissions, and other economic bodies also generally have many more capable staff compared with two decades ago. Many ministries of finance and central banks are now run by competent, world-class professionals who have charted out far more sensible and balanced approaches for the future. As Paul Collier has aptly put it, they have learned from the mistakes of the past and are not likely to repeat them. A perfect example is Benno Ndulu, lead author of the AERC growth project and now the governor of the Central Bank of Tanzania. A coauthor of the study, Chukwuma Soludo, was until recently governor of the Central Bank of Nigeria. And there are many more. Much has been made over the years of the importance of the technical competence of economic policymakers in the Asian "miracle" countries, and rightly so. In the last 15 years, Africa has begun to develop a cadre of its own professionals that are now in senior positions, with at least some independence for sound policymaking.

At the same time, the shift toward democracy, greater transparency, and increased accountability has fundamentally changed the dynamic for the formation of public policies. The press is freer and livelier in many countries, and there are a growing number of NGOs, think tanks, business groups, and other organizations that push for more sensible economic and social policies. A new generation has come of age that expects and demands competent economic management. Today, younger entrepreneurs and members of a small but growing middle class, many with experience living internationally and with global connections through cell phones and the internet, are pushing for practical solutions to problems and a more accountable leadership, as discussed in Chapter 7. Most of today's leaders and technocrats in the emerging countries are more responsive to their citizens and concerned about a wider range of development issues, broad-based economic growth, and poverty reduction.

The stronger economic management in conjunction with the rise of democracy has been a surprise to some: there was concern in the mid-1990s that as African countries became more democratic, policies would deteriorate in response to multiple interests and populist pressures. But this has not been the case. Rather, the shift toward more democratic governance appears to have (imperfectly) increased accountability and significantly improved economic management relative to authoritarian governments. Leaders today are not simply responding to the interests of a narrow range of supporters through patronage politics, at least not to the extent of the past, but instead are responding to the need for sensible economic policies for a broader segment of the population.

This all bodes well for the future. The combination of stronger economic leadership, learning from the past, increased public pressure for sensible economic policies, and greater accountability is critically important. It provides greater confidence that the improved economic policies of the last decade can be sustained and further strengthened. There will be mistakes and setbacks, as there are anywhere. But with strong economic leadership and accountability mechanisms, governments in the emerging countries are likely to implement sound economic policies that will continue, slowly but surely, to provide the foundation for sustained economic growth and poverty reduction in the future.

Former World Bank President James D. Wolfensehn and World Bank Managing Director Ngozi Okonjo-Iweala at the 2009 World Bank/IMF Annual Meetings (© Simone D. McCourtie/World Bank)

5

The END of the **DEBT CRISIS** and **CHANGING RELATIONSHIPS** with DONORS

On August 12, 1982, Mexican Finance Minister Jesús Silva Herzog shocked the financial world by announcing that Mexico could no longer service its debts. Within weeks, international banks began withdrawing lines of credit and cutting their exposure to developing countries around the world. Suddenly, many developing countries faced an enormous credit squeeze, making it enormously difficult to service older loans. What became known as the 1980s debt crisis was under way.

The debt crisis had its roots in the oil price shocks, volatile commodity prices, and deep global recession of the late 1970s and early 1980s. The impacts were worsened by the poor policy responses of many governments (described in the previous chapter) and by the poor lending decisions of aggressive creditors—both rich governments and commercial banks—that lent far too much money to dictators and badly managed countries.

The crisis took a heavy toll. The 1980s became Latin America's "lost decade," with economic growth slowing from 6 percent to 1 percent. Countries around the world were engulfed in the crisis, including Argentina, Chile, Bolivia, Brazil, Jordan, Nigeria, Peru, the Philippines, Venezuela, and many others. Even some high-flyers like South Korea and Indonesia faced problems. The average debt-to-export ratio for developing countries more than tripled, from 127 percent to 463 percent between 1970 and 1986. By that time, 72 countries had debt-to-export ratios greater than 150 percent. With the combination of the global recession and the debt crisis, economic growth plunged in developing countries around the world, and poverty soared.

Critically, the crisis also fundamentally changed the relationships between donors and developing countries. Perhaps the biggest change was the emergence of the International Monetary Fund as a dominant actor, through both its financing and its role in establishing policy conditions that became the basis for the vast majority of donor funding. The IMF, together with the World Bank, in effect became the donors' "gatekeepers": only if a country continued to meet the IMF's and World Bank's conditions were donors willing to provide significant financial support, including debt rescheduling and (later) debt reduction. Thus, because of the debt crisis, many developing countries, especially the most indebted ones, lost a large measure of independence in setting their own policy agendas. In some countries, this was not altogether a bad thing, given the abysmal policies that they had been following. But in many cases, conditionality went much too far, with donors controlling the agenda with little input from, or accountability to, the citizens of the countries themselves.

By the early 1990s, the debt crisis was beginning to be resolved for some countries, mainly middle-income countries that had borrowed primarily from commercial banks. But for low-income countries, including most African countries, the crisis went on for another decade or more. Only through the Heavily Indebted Poor Country (HIPC) Initiative and the Multilateral Debt Relief Initiative (MDRI) were most low-income countries finally able to come out from under the debt burden, in most cases only beginning in 1999 or later.

Today, of the 40 countries eligible for the HIPC program—the residual group of countries ensnared in the crisis—36 have received at least the first stage of HIPC debt relief, leaving just 4 of the most difficult cases to go.[1] Twenty-nine countries have completed the entire process. Thus, while the crisis still lingers in a few countries, for most the 1980s debt crisis is finally over.

Critically, just as the run-up in debt changed the relationship with the donors, the resolution of the debt crisis has changed the donor relationship once again. The dominant role of the IMF and the World Bank in establishing many key policies is receding (slowly). IMF and World Bank "stabilization" and "structural adjustment" programs have been replaced at the center of the dialogue by country-led poverty reduction and development strategies. Developing countries must no longer continually go

---

1 The four remaining countries that are eligible for the HIPC initiative but have not qualified for the first stage of debt relief as of July 2010 are Eritrea, the Kyrgyz Republic, Somalia, and Sudan.

back to donors to ask for another round of (conditional) debt restructuring. The balance today between country-led policies and donor input is far from perfect, but it has shifted markedly over the last decade. In Africa, this is particularly true in the emerging countries that have begun to establish a record of good governance and strong economic policy management.

The end of the debt crisis brings with it three key changes that bode well for the future. First, debt service payment obligations have decreased, relieving pressure on the budget and bringing direct economic benefits. Second, policymakers can focus more of their time and attention on important policy issues at home rather than spend time constantly renegotiating debts and the accompanying conditions. Third, the end of the crisis has created a healthier relationship between developing countries and donors.

Some commentators and analysts worry that certain countries may begin to borrow heavily and slip back into a new debt crisis. It may be that some countries will face renewed debt difficulties in the future. But with few exceptions the amount of new borrowing in recent years has remained very modest, and by and large the funds are being used for worthwhile investments that can support long-term growth. Moreover, the combination of the end of the crisis, the changed relationship with donors, improved economic policies, and stronger governance has created, especially in the emerging countries, a much more solid foundation for managing their economies and sustaining economic growth in the years to come.

The Debt Crisis and Donor Conditionality in Africa

By the mid-1980s, most countries in SSA were experiencing debt difficulties, and these problems were at the center of the economic crisis that plagued the continent between 1975 and 1995. The average debt-to-export ratio in SSA rose from 92 percent to an enormous 651 percent between 1970 and 1986, and 36 countries had debt-to-export ratios exceeding 150 percent. Some countries, such as Liberia, outright defaulted on their debt and remained in default for years. Others avoided default, but only by cutting back on consumption and investment and by pleading with donors either to reschedule their debts repeatedly or to provide new loans to repay old ones. Government budgets were squeezed, with debt service eating up one-third or more of revenues in some countries, leading to cutbacks in health, education, infrastructure, civil service salaries, and a variety of other government services. Maintenance on infrastructure took a particularly large hit in many countries. Partly because of the debt burden, investment in SSA fell by about 15 percent in real terms from 1974–82 to 1983–93 and weakened the foundation for future growth.

At the same time, the crisis dramatically changed the role of the donors, particularly the IMF and the World Bank. In the 1980s, both began providing "structural adjustment" loans with low interest rates and long repayment periods that allowed countries to repay higher interest loans, and thereby provided some measure of debt relief. But the quid pro quo for these loans was that recipients had to introduce a long list of economic and governance conditions. Through this process, the IMF and World Bank took on a central role in setting the policy and development agenda in developing countries. Their influence was magnified because other donors looked to them to establish their own policy reform frameworks and conditioned their aid flows and debt restructurings on the basis of how well countries performed on IMF and World Bank programs. World Bank loans would not go forward in the absence of a satisfactory IMF program, and a prerequisite for debt rescheduling and partial forgiveness from the Paris Club—the informal group of bilateral government creditors—was adhering to the conditions of an IMF program.

IMF conditionality was highly controversial, with debates raging on the scope of the reforms, the degree of input from local actors, the extent to which they actually led to policy reform, and their efficacy in improving outcomes. The IMF deserves a little more slack than it often receives; it is important to bear in mind that it only is invited into a country when the situation is so bad that other financing options are gone and all choices involve hardships. The IMF is an easy scapegoat. And it deserves some credit: many of the policies it pushed for—more sensible exchange rates, smaller budget deficits, lower tariff rates, and less egregious state involvement in the economy—were important steps in the right direction and eventually contributed to the turnaround in the emerging countries.

Nevertheless, government officials and civil society groups viewed both the IMF and World Bank as inflexible, unwilling to discuss options, focused too much on short-term stabilization rather than long-term growth and development, and too often driven by the ideology of their major shareholders rather than the practical realities on the ground. And while reform packages were generally in the right direction, they were at times overly restrictive on fiscal policies and had negative consequences on health, education, and other social sectors; too aggressive on the pace of privatization, pushing for replacing public monopolies with private ones even in the absence of strong regulatory environments; and overzealous on trade liberalization. Ministers of finance and other government officials spent huge amounts of time negotiating conditions and meeting with visiting missions, a process that was repeated multiple times a year for many years.

The debates about IMF and World Bank conditionality were the leading edge of a broader debate about the role of donors and the effectiveness of aid in Africa. The combination of poor economic performance and irresponsible governance in so many countries led taxpayers in many donor countries to become skeptical of aid, and for donors to be much more directive in determining both what aid would be used for and how it would be delivered. Aid flows became heavily earmarked to match the donor's highest priorities rather than those of the recipient, and programs were increasingly designed by donors rather than recipients. And as corruption spread within dictatorial and unaccountable governments, donors—not surprisingly—shifted to delivering aid through contractors and NGOs rather than through government institutions. Donor focus shifted away from achieving strong development results toward safely accounting for how every dollar was spent.

To an extent, some of these changes were understandable, given the poor leadership and rampant corruption in so many countries, especially in the 1980s. But while they may have protected donor funds, they had several downsides. They further weakened governance in recipient countries by drawing some of the most able professionals out of government to work for aid agencies, contractors, and NGOs. They were applied uniformly across all countries, even those that were relatively better governed. And they established rigid structures in donor organizations that have proved difficult to change, even as the conditions in many African countries have changed significantly. When the Cold War ended in 1990, aid flows dropped sharply. Globally, aid fell about 25 percent in real terms between 1991 and 1997. In SSA, the drop was even larger, with aid falling fully one-third in real terms between the peak in 1990 and the nadir in 1999.

But both the support for aid in donor countries and the mechanisms through which aid is delivered began to change again—this time in a more positive direction—starting in the late 1990s. And once again the changes were deeply intertwined with the debt crisis, this time as the debt crisis finally began to be resolved two decades after it had started.

Resolving the Debt Crisis

The resolution of the debt crisis has evolved in three stages over the last two decades. First, private creditors agreed to partial debt reduction and broader restructuring in some countries, mostly middle-income, under the umbrella of the Brady Plan beginning in 1989. Second, at about the same time, government creditors, under the auspices of the so-called Paris Club, began to offer partial write-downs combined with rescheduling for low-income countries, so long as they were meeting economic conditions as part of an IMF program. The Paris Club progressively increased the extent of debt relief it offered throughout the 1990s, ultimately reaching 90 percent net present value reduction in 1999 under the so-called Cologne terms. Today, many government creditors offer 100 percent debt relief to qualifying low-income countries.

The third stage was the Heavily Indebted Poor Country (HIPC) Initiative, which was a combined effort of the major multilateral (the IMF, World Bank, African Development Bank, and others) and bilateral creditors. The HIPC Initiative marked the first time ever that multilateral institutions had provided debt reduction. It has evolved in three stages: (1) the original program in 1996; (2) the "enhanced" HIPC Initiative in 1999, which deepened the extent of debt relief; and (3) the Multilateral Debt Relief Initiative (MDRI) in 2005, which, while technically separate from HIPC, provides 100 percent debt relief to qualifying countries on debts owed to the major multilaterals. Critically, as with Brady and Paris Club deals, maintaining performance on a high-conditionality IMF program is a core requirement for countries to receive HIPC debt relief.

Thirty-three African countries are eligible for HIPC and MDRI. By mid-2010, 22 of them had completed the full process and received substantial debt reduction, and 8 others had reached a first stage and were receiving interim debt relief. Three more countries remain eligible, but have not met the requirements to begin the process (Eritrea, Somalia, and Sudan). In addition, a few other countries have benefited from significant debt relief outside of the HIPC process, most notably Nigeria.

As a result of these initiatives, debt burdens in SSA today are substantially lower than in the 1990s. Whereas the average debt-to-export ratio grew by a factor of six from 92 percent in 1970 to 644 percent in 1994, it has since fallen sharply to reach just 192 percent in 2007 (Figure 5.1). Whereas debt service payments required 16 percent of export earnings in 1995, today they require less than 8 percent, freeing up valuable resources that can be spent on infrastructure, health, education, or other high-priority needs, or used to close budget deficits or increase foreign exchange reserves.

A central question, of course, is whether countries will begin to borrow heavily and find themselves in debt difficulties again in the future. Some new borrowing is perfectly sensible, especially if it is on concessional terms and used for investments that support economic growth, such as for roads and power. Most African countries have huge infrastructure deficits that limit growth and poverty reduction, and grant funding alone

FIGURE 5.1 Debt Burdens Have Fallen Sharply since the mid-1990s
External Debt as a Share of Exports

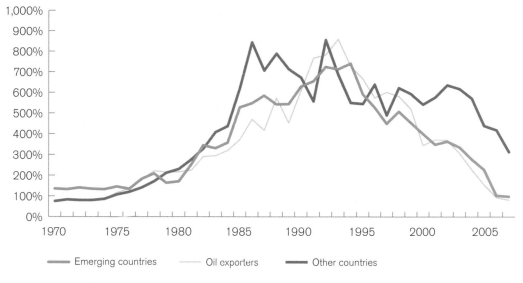

Source: World Bank, World Development Indicators.

will be insufficient to meet these needs. Too little borrowing will undermine growth and poverty reduction. But too much borrowing for the wrong purposes and in the wrong circumstances will mean a return to trouble. The keys will be to limit new borrowing to prudent levels, borrow on concessional terms to the extent possible, use the funds for productive investments, report all borrowing—including off-balance-sheet guarantees—regularly and publicly alongside debt sustainability indicators, and maintain strong economic management to keep growth on track.

Some African countries will probably face debt difficulties again, most likely as a result of some combination of poor economic management and bad luck. This may even be true for some of the emerging countries. After all, almost all rich and middle-income countries have experienced debt problems at one time or another, and most have been repeat customers.

But a return to widespread debt difficulties in the emerging countries in the next decade or more seems unlikely. The 1980s debt crisis was brought on by a lethal combination of poor economic management, unaccountable and highly corrupt governments, large amounts of borrowing at market rates, and a deep global economic shock. The 2009 global financial crisis was the worst shock to the world economy in decades. But overall, the emerging countries responded fairly well to the crisis with appropriate policy responses, and for the most part are maintaining positive economic growth. Going forward, so long as the prudent economic management and stronger governance that helped bring about the turnaround in the emerging countries continue—that is, so long as there is not a fundamental reversal back to weaker governance and poor economic policy—the emerging countries should be in a good position to avoid a return to major debt difficulties in the future.

In addition to better economic circumstances, the end of the 1980s debt crisis brought with it significant changes in the relationship between SSA countries and donors and international agencies, in particular changes in the role of the IMF and World Bank. By the late 1990s, many emerging countries had been implementing relatively strong macroeconomic programs for a decade. They were no longer in need of emergency IMF financing. Instead, they needed the IMF primarily for a very different purpose: to obtain the Fund's "seal of approval" as the gateway to debt relief and other donor assistance. And so it was that by the late 1990s the centerpiece of countries' relationships with the donor community shifted from stabilization and structural adjustment programs to the requirements for debt relief.

But this is changing again. Now that countries are completing the debt relief process, they do not need high-conditionality programs or the IMF's seal of approval. The new relationship is still evolving, but some new characteristics are clear. Donors are putting a greater focus on allowing recipient countries to set priorities and design programs and on achieving clear results rather than strong conditionality. The focus of debate has shifted from IMF programs to the country's own poverty reduction strategies, in which it can set out its priorities, plans, and programs. But before going into more detail on these changes, let's first examine the broader debate on aid effectiveness, since it is intertwined with debt relief and the changes in conditionality and other donor practices.

The Aid Effectiveness Debate

There are many strong views about aid in Africa. Proponents see aid as an important supporting tool that can accelerate the pace of development and poverty reduction, especially in countries with strong economic policies and good governance. Critics argue that aid has done little good and at best has been ineffective. Some have gone further and argued that aid is actually the cause of Africa's underdevelopment.

The critics make some important points. They argue that despite several decades of aid flows, growth in Africa has languished (although they usually fail to recognize the change in growth since the mid-1990s, or that private investment also failed to spur growth and often facilitated corruption and propped up bad governments even more than aid did). They show that significant amounts of funding are lost along the way to overly complex bureaucracies or to poorly designed projects with little chance of success. They argue that much aid has been delivered with little input from local citizens and intended beneficiaries, leading to poor design, a lack of local understanding of what is being done and why, and less local commitment to making projects succeed. They point out that under certain circumstances aid can undermine private investment by causing the local currency to appreciate—the so-called Dutch Disease effect—which reduces profits for exporters and slows growth and economic diversification (at least if aid is not used in investments aimed at reducing production costs through building infrastructure and other related areas).

They also argue, correctly, that at times donors have used aid to prop up dangerous dictators who did enormous damage, especially in the 1980s and early 1990s during the height of the Cold War. This critique is less about the effectiveness of aid per se than the wisdom of broader foreign policy goals—not directly related to development—for which rich countries supported unaccountable, undemocratic dictators. The bad idea here was not so much aid as it was supporting terrible governments. Nevertheless, these practices contributed substantially to the negative record of aid.

But many critics go too far and overstate their case. Although there have been many failures of aid, there have been many successes that receive much less attention. Some of Africa's most successful countries have been large aid recipients, starting with Botswana and Mauritius. Botswana received assistance averaging more than US$150 per person (in today's dollars) for more than 30 years, more than *triple* the average for the rest of the continent, assistance which helped build infrastructure and support health and education programs. Mauritius received aid averaging more than US$65 per person for 30 years, which helped it build some of the infrastructure and services that made it successful. Since 1993, Mozambique's GDP has grown more than 7.5 percent per year and its poverty rate has dropped substantially, supported by assistance averaging US$60 per person per year. Rwanda, Tanzania, Uganda, and several other countries have achieved rapid growth since the mid-1990s while receiving relatively large amounts of aid. In Liberia, since the end of the long civil war in 2003, assistance has been instrumental in helping maintain peace, rebuild crumbling infrastructure, recruit talent, and finance health and education programs. As President Sirleaf notes in the introduction to this book, without this assistance, Liberia easily could have slipped back to war.

Foreign assistance has helped finance investments in education, water, agriculture, and, perhaps most clearly, in health (indeed, some of the harshest critics of aid have had to backpedal and recognize the contribution of aid in improving health). Funding for HIV/AIDS programs, primarily from the United States and the Global Fund to Fights Aids, Tuberculosis and Malaria, has helped put 2.5 million Africans on life-saving antiretroviral treatment. Aid-supported programs have helped control river blindness and polio, among other diseases, and helped eradicate smallpox. And donor-financed programs have helped vaccinate millions of children every year, developed a simple sugar and salt tablet that helps control diarrhea, and today are helping to control the scourge of malaria. Without these and similar programs, millions more Africans would die every year.[2]

Across the emerging African countries, with the economic and political turnaround since the mid-1990s, the prototypical negative view that despite large amounts of aid Africa is making no progress is simply out of date and inaccurate. These countries have made lots of progress since the mid-1990s, as we have shown. Critically, in these countries aid was not the most important ingredient behind their success; strong leadership, good governance, and sensible polices were the foundation. Aid did not ignite the initial turnaround, but it has played an important secondary role in helping to support and sustain their progress over time.

So how do the successes and failures balance out? While a few research studies have found no relationship between aid and development outcomes, most research tends to find an overall modest positive relationship.[3] With respect to economic growth, Paul Collier summarized it about right in *The Bottom Billion:* "A reasonable estimate is that over the last thirty years [aid] has added around one percentage point to the annual growth rate of the bottom billion."[4] Other work has shown a modest positive impact on other development outcomes, particularly health. Research has shown the benefits of deworming tablets in getting kids in school, oral rehydration therapy in fighting childhood diarrhea, childhood immunization programs in fighting disease, and "cash transfer" programs that in effect pay parents to keep their kids in school, to name a few.

It is time to move away from the strong caricatures on both sides of this debate. Aid is neither the panacea nor the demon it is sometimes made out to be. It is not the most important driver of growth and development; it is secondary to capable leadership, good governance, peace and stability, and sensible economic and social policies. But it can play an important supporting role in helping to achieve important development outcomes.

---

2 For an excellent analysis of achievements in the health sector, see Ruth Levine, et al., *Millions Saved: Proven Successes in Global Health* (Washington, DC: Center for Global Development, 2004).

3 For a summary of the research, see Steven Radelet, "Foreign Aid," in *International Handbook of Development Economics,* ed. Amitava Dutt and Jamie Ros (London: Edward Elgar, 2008).

4 Paul Collier, *The Bottom Billion: Why the Poorest Countries Are Failing and What Can Be Done About It* (New York: Oxford University Press, 2007).

Nevertheless, no one should be satisfied with business as usual. There is enormous room for improvement. Fortunately, the debate on aid has begun to move beyond the simple (and unhelpful), extreme views to focus on better understanding when and where aid can work, and how assistance programs can be strengthened to support development better. The basic challenge for donors and their partners is to find ways to support communities and governments in achieving important development outcomes with a minimum of bureaucracy and intrusion, but also with appropriate oversight to minimize the loss of funds and to measure results. Fortunately, aid programs have begun to evolve, slowly but perceptibly, in response to these challenges, and thus have been better able to support the economic resurgence in the emerging countries in recent years. We now turn to look at some of these changes.

New Directions in Foreign Assistance

As the debt crisis has wound down, donors have begun to introduce important changes in their aid programs, especially in the emerging countries and others that have begun moving toward more capable governance. While some of these changes are still in their early stages, and donors can do much more to improve aid effectiveness, the landscape has changed significantly over the last decade and continues to evolve in constructive ways.

First, IMF programs are no longer at the center of the donor-recipient relationship and have been replaced (in post-HIPC countries) by poverty reduction strategies (PRSs), formulated and developed by countries themselves. These strategies differ fundamentally from IMF programs in the inclusive process used in most cases to develop them, their broader focus on poverty reduction, and their strategic focus. At first, some of the early poverty reductions strategies were less than satisfactory in both process and content. Some countries just went through the motions to satisfy the donors as a requirement for HIPC debt relief. Too often, donors themselves were more than happy to just write a PRS on behalf of a government, or tell them exactly what to do. For example, the World Bank issued a 1,260-page "sourcebook" as a reference to "guide" countries developing these strategies.

But the PRSs have become much stronger in recent years. Most countries have found them very valuable, both as a way to engender debate and consensus on policies and as a guide for policy decisions, the allocation of resources, and progress toward specific goals. Many countries have continued to update and renew their PRSs, even after they were no longer required to do so by the donors as part of the debt relief process.

The key point is that these country-led PRSs—as imperfect as they sometimes are—have largely replaced stabilization and structural adjustment programs and have shifted the balance toward countries establishing key policies and priorities themselves. This has been especially evident in better-governed countries, including the emerging African countries, that have shown the capacity to develop sound strategies and set sensible priorities. The PRSs are far from perfect, but they are a major step forward in redefining the relationship between recipients and donors.

Second, the IMF has begun to alter its approach, reducing the extent of its policy conditions and focusing more on policy dialogue. It introduced the Policy Support Instrument (PSI) in 2005, a new type of program for countries like the emerging countries with solid macroeconomic policies that do not require significant policy reform, IMF funding, or debt relief, but want a mechanism for active and ongoing policy discussions with the IMF. For low-income countries that do require financing, in response to the global financial crisis, the IMF in 2009 increased the amount of financing available, lowered its interest rates, and introduced several new facilities tailored for different circumstances. Critically, it streamlined the required conditions in many of its programs by focusing more on core issues and providing more flexibility on structural reform conditions. In most cases, these programs are much more aligned and consistent with a country's own PRS and macroeconomic framework than were IMF programs of the past.

Just as the IMF's role changed as the debt crisis emerged in the 1980s, it is changing again as the debt crisis finally wanes. Going forward, for the emerging African countries and others that have adopted strong economic policies and do not require debt relief, the IMF's relevance increasingly will depend on its ability to provide high-quality policy advice that countries value rather than on its ability to enforce certain policies or directly influence funding and debt relief. These countries are in a stronger position to decide the kind of relationship they want with the IMF, and they will increasingly base their decisions on their judgment of the usefulness of the IMF's advice. It remains to be seen how much these recent developments represent real change, but they are moving in a promising new direction and provide the basis for a healthier and more balanced relationship between better-governed countries and the IMF.

Third, donors have begun to adjust some of their approaches by creating new programs and changing traditional programs. The most prominent of the new initiatives are the Global Fund to Fight AIDS, Tuberculosis and Malaria; the Millennium Challenge Corporation (MCC); and the GAVI Alliance (formerly the Global Alliance for Vaccines and Immunizations). Each focuses on programs designed in the recipient country through a consultative process rather than programs designed by donors. They are all more results-oriented than traditional approaches, with clearly specified goals against which to measure progress. The MCC adds the further distinction of being highly selective: only countries with a demonstrated record of good governance and strong economic and social policies, like most of the emerging African countries, are eligible for MCC funding. Not surprisingly, there is significant overlap between the emerging countries and MCC countries. Of the 17 emerging African countries, 13 have incomes low enough to be considered by the MCC for funding (the exceptions are Botswana, Mauritius, the Seychelles, and South Africa, where incomes are too high). Of these 13 countries, the MCC has selected 12 as either fully eligible for its largest programs or for its "threshold" program (Ethiopia is the only exception).

In addition, in recent years several donors have begun to experiment with providing more funding as either direct budget support or through pooled funds supporting specific sectors. When used in the right context, these approaches can help match donor funds better to government priorities, cut through donor bureaucracy so more money gets to the country itself, and help countries strengthen their own budget and procurement processes. There are drawbacks, in particular the difficulty for donors to track their funds precisely, challenges in measuring the impact of these funds, and concerns that funds might be subject to poor oversight or corruption. These approaches have generated considerable debate, and fortunately the debate is moving beyond the simple question of whether they are good or bad and to the more important issues of the circumstances under which they are appropriate, when they are not, and how they can be used to strengthen local capacity and budget institutions. Many of the emerging countries are precisely the places where this kind of support might make most sense.

These new approaches are far from perfect, and the changes in recent years are incomplete. While some donors have begun to try new methods and shift to country-led, results-based approaches, others have not, and in some cases the rhetoric is far ahead of the reality. And there are still too many decisions on priorities and strategies that are determined by the donors, leaving some areas chronically underfunded, most especially agriculture and infrastructure. But there is a clear difference in attitudes and approaches from just a few years ago. These changes are promising steps in the right direction for making aid programs more effective, and they show some willingness by the funders to try new directions and experiment with change.

Fourth, a new wave of private foundations has emerged that is experimenting with new approaches and mechanisms. The Bill and Melinda Gates Foundation has brought new expertise and energy to health programs and agriculture, with a strong focus on technology and achieving measurable results. The Open Society Institute has led the charge in supporting efforts to build transparent and accountable democracies. The William J. Clinton Foundation has helped countries negotiate more favorable prices for drug purchases and is providing welcome support to the health sectors in some countries such as Liberia. The Acumen Fund, the McCall MacBain Foundation, and the Soros Economic Development Fund are working at the intersection of philanthropy and investment, using their funds to leverage private sector investment in small and medium enterprises. The Acumen Fund is investing in a bed net factory in Tanzania; the investment arm of the McCall MacBain Foundation is converting old rubber trees into wood chips for biomass fuel and is building a new biomass power station in Liberia; and the Soros Economic Development Fund is investing in banks and microfinance institutions (among other entities). And the list goes on.

These foundations and philanthropies, most of which did not exist 15 years ago, are bringing new ideas, energy, and expertise to the fore across Africa. They are far more willing to experiment, take risks, and work at the cutting edge of supporting governments, NGOs, and citizen groups. They are important in and of themselves, but they are also providing examples for, and competition with, traditional donors. They are a major force in the drive to make donor funding, public and private, more effective in supporting sustained development in the future.

Fifth, while it is important to make aid more effective, the amount of funding matters and it has been on the rise. After declining sharply in the early 1990s, aid funding for sub-Saharan Africa began to rise again in the late 1990s and has increased significantly in recent years. Total Official Development Assistance for the 17 emerging African countries—including grants and concessional loans, net of debt repayments and one-time debt relief operations—was about US$5.8 billion in 1998 (in today's dollars), slightly less than a decade earlier. But it increased by more than 70 percent in real terms in the decade between 1998 and 2008, reaching US$10 billion.

Critically, a larger share of total funding is in grants rather than loans, helping to reduce the risks of a new debt crisis going forward. Most of the major bilateral donors shifted away from loans to grants in the late 1980s and early 1990s (although some continue to provide primarily loans). And in 2002, the World Bank and the African Development Bank began providing a significant share of their concessional funding as grants rather than loans. In 1988, nearly 20 percent of all official financing to the emerging countries was either market rate or concessional loans. By 2008, the share had fallen to about 6 percent (Figure 5.2).

While these changes are important, aid is—as I have stressed—secondary to strong government policies, effective governance, and other improvements to enhance long-term growth and development. Moreover, it is not the most important policy tool rich countries have to

FIGURE 5.2 More Grants, Fewer Loans

Official Financing for the Emerging African Countries

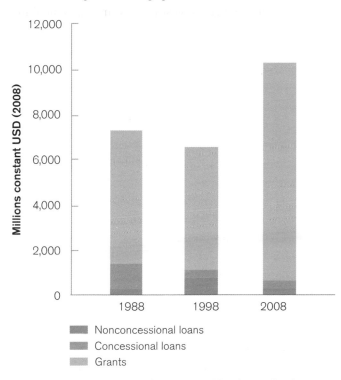

Source: Organisation for Economic Co-operation and Development, Development Assistance Committee database, tables 2a and 2b. Accessed April 24, 2010, http://www.oecd.org/document/33/0.2340.en_2649_34447_36661793_1_1_1_1.00.html.

influence growth and development in the emerging countries. Much greater influence comes through trade and investment policies.

In these key areas, there has been much less progress. Barriers to trade and subsidies for rich-country producers, especially in agriculture, undermine competitive producers in poor countries around the world, including the emerging countries in Africa. These policies retard investment, growth, and poverty reduction. It does little good to preach to poor countries that private sector development and integration with global markets are the keys to development if rich countries continue to subsidize their own firms and restrict trade.

There have been some modest steps forward in reducing certain trade barriers, such as the United States' African Growth and Opportunity Act (AGOA) and the EU's Everything But Arms Initiative. But the massive increase in agricultural subsidies in the United States and other countries in recent years, and the failure of the Doha Round of trade talks, leave a playing field that is skewed against private sector producers in developing countries. While making aid more effective is an important priority, an even higher priority should be given to reducing trade barriers in Europe, Japan, the United States, and other places to give poor country producers an even shake.

* * *

The end of the 25-year debt crisis removes a heavy burden from the shoulders of Africa's emerging economies. Governments can now devote more resources to building roads, schools, and clinics, rather than trying to repay old loans taken on by dictators that badly mismanaged their economies. Their finance ministers can dedicate more of their scarce time and energy to important policy issues at home rather than constantly renegotiating debt. Countries no longer will be seen by the international financial community primarily as debtor deadbeats, but rather as countries that have overcome their past and are re-engaging with global markets on sound footing. And while some countries may find themselves facing debt difficulties again in the future, in the absence of a major reversal in economic management, it seems unlikely that the emerging countries as a group will return to systemic debt troubles again anytime soon.

The changes in approaches by the IMF, World Bank, and other donors, and the greater focus on country-led strategies, have not solved all of the problems that have plagued aid programs. But aid programs have evolved significantly in recent years, and most of the changes have been in the right direction. Donors have shown a willingness and ability to modify their approaches in response to past criticisms of aid. As a result, aid has helped provide important support to the economic revival in many of the emerging countries.

The economic benefits from debt relief and changes in practices by and relationships with the donor community are creating the basis for more effective partnerships going forward. And so they provide another important building block in the foundation for the emerging countries to continue their development renaissance into the future.

6

THE TECHNOLOGY
REVOLUTION

The Song-Taaba Yalgré organization in Burkina Faso had a problem. This vibrant group, made up mostly of women living in remote areas where poverty and illiteracy flourish, had begun to earn some welcome additional income by producing shea butter for export. But their efforts were being undermined by difficulties in getting the information they needed about production needs, deliveries, and prices. Communication was difficult, time-consuming, and costly. How could they better connect their 2,000 rural members with headquarters in the capital of Ouagadougou and exchange accurate information on what, where, and when to sell?

The answer came from something most members had never heard of before: the Internet. When Song-Taaba Yalgré established small information centers with Internet access in two key rural areas of shea butter producers, they were able to improve the flow of information rapidly between the central offices and rural producers. The result was improved efficiency, higher production levels, increased profits, and more women joining in to produce shea butter and earn their own incomes. In the three years after the information centers were introduced, shea butter production by Song-Taaba Yalgré increased sharply, and members received basic training in using computers to market their products more efficiently to regional and international buyers.[1] Today, fully 90 percent of the association's sales are via the Internet. Members also use cell phones and GPS technology to track locations, surface area, numbers of trees, and other field data to harvest shea butter fruit more effectively.

Special thanks to Rebecca Schutte, Molly Kinder, and Casey Dunning for their help researching and drafting sections of this chapter.

1 IICD, "Burkina Faso's Shea Butter Producers Go Online," http://www.iicd.org/articles/logon4d/burkina-faso2019s-shea-butter-producers-go-online/.

"My God! Ten years ago, I wouldn't have ever guessed that I would be writing and using a computer" says Awa Sawadogo, a member who never went to school but now writes the association's newspaper. "Now, I can write in Moré, my mother tongue. I know how to create a folder and a file. . . . For us women from rural areas, [technological] tools mean learning and opening up to the world," she says.[2]

Meanwhile, across the continent in the tiny rural village of Bushenyi, Uganda,

> Laban Rutagumirwa charges his mobile phone with a car battery because his dirt-floor home deep in the remote, banana-covered hills of western Uganda does not have electricity. When the battery dies, Mr. Rutagumirwa, a 50-year-old farmer, walks just over four miles to charge it so he can maintain his position as communication hub and banana-disease tracker for his rural neighbors. In an area where electricity is scarce and Internet connections virtually nonexistent, the mobile phone has revolutionized scientists' ability to track this crop disease and communicate the latest scientific advances to remote farmers. With his phone, Mr. Rutagumirwa collects digital photos, establishes global positioning system coordinates and stores completed 50-question surveys from nearby farmers with sick plants. He sends this data, wirelessly and instantly, to scientists in the Ugandan capital, Kampala. "We never had any idea about getting information with the phone," Mr. Rutagumirwa said. "It was a mystery. Now our mind is wide open." [3]

Today, thanks to the rapid expansion of mobile phones, Internet connections, and other forms of information and communications technology (ICT), the opportunities for technology to help lift people out of poverty and change the economic fortune of Africa have never been greater. Across Africa, mobile phones and Internet connections are expanding economic opportunities, creating jobs, reducing business costs, extending financial networks, strengthening health systems, improving information flows, and increasing transparency and accountability. They are affecting nearly every part of the economy in one way or another, including agriculture, manufacturing, customs clearance, banking, and tourism.

In places with bad roads, no landlines, no hope of a train, and unreliable postal services, mobile phones are opening the world to poor villages, creating unprecedented access to information on prices, market conditions, banking services, legal advice, and medical care. They enable farmers and

---

2 Ramata Soré, "Burkina Faso Shea Butter Producers Go High Tech," IDG News Service, May 15, 2008, http://www.pcworld.com/businesscenter/article/145954/burkina_faso_shea_butter_producers_go_high_tech.html.

3 Sarah Arnquist, "In Rural Africa, a Fertile Market for Mobile Phones," *New York Times*, October 6, 2009, http://www.nytimes.com/2009/10/06/science/06uganda.html.

fishermen to bypass inefficient marketing systems and make higher profits. Innovative text message schemes inform farmers about prices and where and when to sell their crops to maximize their profits. Thousands of poor rural women are using mobile phones and microfinance loans to set up small businesses that charge customers for airtime on the phone. Families are quickly and easily sending remittances by cell phones to relatives in remote villages. Literacy programs dictated over mobile phones are beginning to show promise. Increased Internet connectivity has led to the emergence of data-entry firms that have created thousands of jobs in South Africa, Ghana, and other countries. And, critically, mobile and Internet technologies are strengthening democratic processes and good governance by spreading news bulletins, transmitting voter turnout and ballot information, and encouraging greater transparency of government finances.

These technologies are still very new to Africa. They clearly were not major contributing factors to the economic and political turnaround that swept across the emerging African countries beginning in the early and mid-1990s. But they have had a huge impact in sustaining the progress in recent years. Most important, they are critical for continuing to expand economic opportunities, information flows, and political accountability in the future.

With the spread of mobile phones continuing to grow at rates of 40 percent a year—the highest growth anywhere in the world—Africa's mobile revolution is just starting. Likewise, Internet connectivity, still out of reach for 95 percent of Africans, is poised to expand as new fiber optic cables are brought to the continent and innovative satellite infrastructure deployed. The ICT revolution has unleashed the ingenuity of entrepreneurial Africans to overcome obstacles that have long stymied Africa's economic progress.

The African ICT Explosion

The expansion of mobile technology in Africa has been nothing short of spectacular. Communities that previously had no telecommunications infrastructure have become some of the world's fastest-growing markets for mobile technologies. Many are "leapfrogging" fixed telephones lines entirely. Mobile phones can now be found in far-flung African villages that are beyond the reach of roads, where fixed-line telephone cables are too costly to install.

Africa has become the fastest-growing mobile market in the world. There were already 230 million phone subscriptions in 2007—double the number from just two years before—and the number has grown substantially since then.[4] In the emerging countries, mobile subscriptions jumped from fewer than 4 per 100 people in 2000 to 28 per 100 in 2007, and in the oil-exporting countries the growth has been even faster (Figure 6.1). Nearly 70 percent of the population in the emerging countries is now covered by a cellular network (Figure 6.2).

Internet access has also grown quickly, especially in the emerging countries (Figure 6.3), although it is much less common compared to the ubiquity of mobile phones. Internet access is reaching 50 million users across the continent, a 10-fold increase over 2000, but still just 5 percent of the population. This low access is in part attributable to the unreliability of electricity, low literacy rates (which is much less of an issue with voice features of mobile phones), and steep prices. Web users pay on average US$366 for a month of service, more than 8 times the cost of similar Internet coverage in India and 20 to 40 times higher than in the United States.[5]

But these high costs are almost certain to drop sharply in the next few years; when they do, Internet access has the potential to expand rapidly. In eastern Africa, the Seacom cable became operational in July 2009 and now provides Internet service that is about 10 times faster than any other service in Africa.[6] In addition, four undersea fiber optic cables are currently under construction on Africa's east coast, including the highly anticipated East African Submarine Cable System, which began operations in mid-2010 and will connect 19 countries between South Africa and Sudan with the rest of the world. West Africa currently has the SAT-3 cable, but it will soon be joined by two more fiber optic cables being built off the West African coast. These cables should significantly increase access and lower costs in capitals and other major coastal cities.

Complementing these efforts is continued rapid expansion of satellite communication, which will provide options for remote areas not immediately hooked to cables. For example, the O3b Network (short for Other Three Billion) is on course to launch a network of 16 low-earth-orbit communications satellites by the end of 2010 with the aim of providing Internet access to 3 billion people in developing countries around the world. The new cables and satellite connections will not solve all the challenges that restrain Internet access, including illiteracy, lack of reliable electricity,

---

4 Matthew Reed, "Africa, World's Fastest Growing Mobile Market," *Vanguard* 28 (April 2008), available at http://allafrica.com/stories/200804280943.html [subscription].

5 Mohsen Khalil, Philippe Dongier, and Christine Zhen-Wei Qiang, eds., *Information and Communications for Development 2009: Extending Reach and Increasing Impact* (Washington, DC: World Bank, 2009), 51.

6 Cat Contiguglia, "With Cable, Laying a Basis for Growth in Africa," *New York Times,* August 10, 2009, http://www.nytimes.com/2009/08/10/business/global/10cable.htm.

**FIGURE 6.1 Mobile Phones Are
Now Everywhere**

Mobile Subscriptions per 100 People

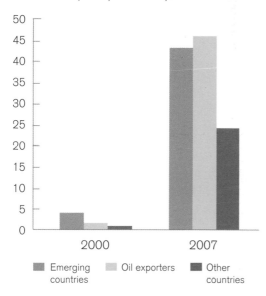

**FIGURE 6.2 . . . and Coverage
Is Widespread**

Population Covered by Cellular Network

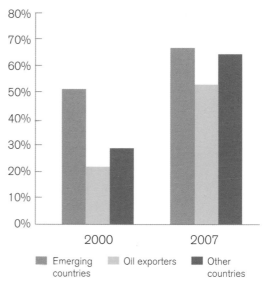

**FIGURE 6.3 Internet Subscriptions Are
Rising . . .**

Internet Subscriptions per 100 People

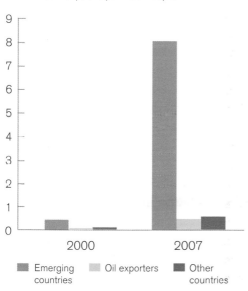

**FIGURE 6.4 . . . and Secure Internet Servers
Are Increasing**

Secure Internet Servers per Million People

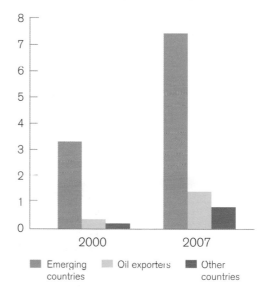

Source: World Bank, Information and Communications for Development 2009: Extending Reach and Increasing Impact,
http://go.worldbank.org/NATLOH7HV0.

and bringing access "the last mile" from the cables to homes and businesses, but they will be major steps forward. The impact of the Internet is certain to continue to grow rapidly, creating new opportunities for economic growth, business creation, education, transparency, and accountability.

Fueling Entrepreneurship and Commerce

As the mobile revolution puts cell phones in the hands of millions of Africans, the possibilities for economic development, improved livelihoods, and raised living standards are enormous. Here is why: in rich countries, mobile phones are an upgrade from relatively reliable land lines to wider coverage with mobile phones, but in many poor countries, especially in rural areas, they are an enormous leap from isolation to instant access to the world. Moreover, the emerging countries have begun to establish the broader economic environment in which these technologies can have huge influence. Mobile technologies help entrepreneurs find customers, order materials, and reduce idle and wasted time, and otherwise bolster the efficiency and productivity of small-scale enterprises. They help make entirely new businesses viable and allow suppliers and customers to create new markets where none existed before.

As Iqbal Quadir, the founder of Grameen Phone, has observed, connectivity is productivity. There is perhaps no greater testament to the dynamic potential of mobile phones than the myriad innovative ways that African entrepreneurs have used mobile technology to bolster their productivity and expand their businesses. From matatu drivers to bricklayers to small shop owners, entrepreneurs and the self-employed are increasingly using mobile phones to spur their business efforts. Construction workers can order supplies with their mobile phones instead of leaving their sites and traveling long distances to stores. Shop owners can place orders for delivery over the phone, instead of shutting their doors during peak hours to run special errands for customers, bolstering their sales potential and profits and reducing wasted time. Electricians and plumbers don't have to return to the shop to retrieve messages about the next job. And instead of sitting idly for hours waiting for customers to offer them work, contract and day laborers can advertise their mobile phone numbers or simply post their numbers on a fixed site.

A particularly dynamic example is Village Phone Operators (VPOs), which were introduced to Uganda through a joint venture by the Grameen Foundation & MTN Uganda. Grassroots entrepreneurs, the VPOs, borrow money from microfinance institutions to purchase their "business in a box"—a mobile phone, which they rent to villagers who wish to place calls. The proceeds from these sales allow VPOs to turn a small profit and repay their loans. VPOs, many of whom are women, typically sell five times the average customer's minute usage, illustrating their role in expanding the reach of mobile phones to new markets. Mary Wokhwale, a great-grandmother in the small village of Bukaweak in eastern Uganda, is a typical example:

> "My mobile phone has been my livelihood," she says. In 2003, Ms. Wokhwale was one of the first 15 women in Uganda to become "village phone" operators. Thanks to a microfinance loan, she was able to buy a basic handset and a roof-mounted antenna to ensure a reliable signal. She went into business selling phone calls to other villagers, making a small profit on each call. This enabled her to pay back her loan and buy a second phone. The income from selling phone calls subsequently enabled her to set up a business selling beer, open a music and video shop and help members of her family pay their children's school fees. . . . Ms. Wokhwale's life has been transformed.[7]

Mobile phones are supporting agriculture by providing much more timely and accurate information to farmers and buyers with much lower transaction costs. Farmers face a major disadvantage because of lack of information on weather, pricing, and market conditions, which undermines their bargaining power and leverage. Without the ability to access market information, farmers often have to travel long distances, at great expense and time, to reach a market, without knowing whether this market will offer the farmer the best price.

But mobile technology is helping farmers overcome these constraints by lowering transaction and search costs, improving coordination, and making markets more efficient and transparent. In Kenya, for instance, the Kenya Agricultural Commodity Exchange (KACE), a private firm, has teamed with mobile provider Safaricom to deliver price and market information to Kenyan farmers. KACE installs information kiosks near commodity markets, collects market information at the kiosks, and disseminates this information through SMS messages to farmers, buyers, and exporters.

Ghana-based TradeNet has been called the eBay of agricultural products. TradeNet matches buyers and sellers of crops across a dozen West African countries. It allows sellers to list their products and an asking price and buyers to indicate what they are looking for at what cost. The information is listed on TradeNet's Web site and is sent to subscribers in one of four languages, creating a virtual market for buyers and sellers to find each other and negotiate a deal.

---

7 "Mobile Marvels," Mobile Marvels: A Special Report on Telecoms in Emerging Markets, *The Economist*, September 26, 2009, 1.

Similarly, in Senegal, Xam Marse, which means "know your market" in Wolof, allows farmers to access real-time, location-specific market information about fruit, vegetables, meat, and poultry through free, daily SMS messages and the Internet. One estimate suggests that farmers who have subscribed to the service have earned 15 percent higher net profits. In Uganda, the Women of Uganda Network collects market price information and sends free SMS texts to 400 farmers. In Niger, a study by Tufts University's Jenny Aker found that the introduction of mobile phones was associated with a 20 percent reduction in grain price differences across markets.[8] As a result, consumer prices were lower and profits were higher. The effects were most dramatic for the least accessible markets. And there are many other examples.

These schemes have not been without challenges, one of which is illiteracy. Some of the programs are getting around this by offering alternatives to text messages. The KACE program in Kenya, for instance, offers farmers the option of receiving the information via voice mail. And NGOs such as World Education are piloting literacy programs using mobile phones to help people learn the alphabet and lists of basic vocabulary words. Another challenge is sustainability. Many of the programs offer information to farmers at no cost, and many farmers do not expect to pay. For the longer-term sustainability of the schemes, however, the value of the information must be clear so that customers are willing to pay for the service.

Beyond agriculture, the mobile phone industry itself is an important source of livelihoods and entrepreneurship. A 2008 World Bank study reported that the mobile industry has spawned 3.5 million jobs in Africa.[9] In 2008, the CEO of Kenya's Safaricom reported that the company directly employed 1,600 employees and indirectly supported an additional 400

---

8 Jenny Aker, "Does Digital Divide or Provide? The Impact of Cell Phones on Grain Providers in Niger," Center for Global Development Working Paper No. 154, http://www.cgdev.org/content/publications/detail/894410/.

9 Asheeta Bhavnani et al.,"The Role of Mobile Phones in Sustainable Poverty Reduction" (Washington, D.C.: World Bank, 2008), http://siteresources.worldbank.org/EXTINFORMATIONANDCOMMUNICATIONANDTECHNOLOGIES/Resources/The_Role_of_Mobile_Phones_in_Sustainable_Rural_Poverty_Reduction_June_2008.pdf.

airtime dealers and 4,000 money transfer dealers. Each of these dealers in turn worked with subdealers, which have their own subdealers, adding up to an extensive distribution channel employing thousands of people. The mobile industry has spawned a wide range of entrepreneurial activities, from self-employed street vendors, who charge phones for a small fee; phone card vendors; mobile phone repair shops; sellers of second-hand handsets; village phone operators; and even "mobile" mobile entrepreneurs, who affix mobile phones and extra batteries to the front of bikes. These kinds of economic opportunities simply did not exist 10 years ago, and they are just the threshold of an even wider range of opportunities in the years to come.

Meanwhile, Internet connectivity is enabling the launch of new services and connections. It enables producers to connect with buyers in other countries, such as Song-Taaba Yalgré's shea butter producers matching up to export markets. The Internet is making it easier for tourists to find hotels and tour opportunities in many countries. One of the most promising areas is outsourcing for data entry and related activities, including call centers. Outsourcing business services tend to be labor-intensive, create a high percentage of jobs for women, and require less capital investment to start than other sectors. Not surprisingly, South Africa has become the major destination for Internet business services, but it is far from alone. Ghana's Internet services sector has created 37,000 direct jobs and 150,000 indirect jobs, and has generated US$750 million in revenues over 5 years.[10] There are clearly constraints; these activities are heavily dependent on ICT infrastructure, including Internet connectivity, reliable power, and to a lesser degree transport infrastructure, all of which are formidable obstacles in many parts of Africa. Even so, the London-based Datamonitor group has forecast that Africa will soon have the fastest-growing call center industry in the world, citing in particular Botswana, Kenya, and Ghana for promising growth.[11]

Expanding Access to Finance

The vast majority of Africans have never set foot in a bank. For many, there is simply no bank branch in their remote communities. For others, the barrier is their own poverty—their desired transactions are too small or too risky for traditional banks to consider. As a result, millions of peo-

---

10 World Bank, "ICT Provides Additional Growth for Ghana," March 8, 2007, http://go.worldbank.org/ KHCVWNRZX0.

11 Rob Crilly, "World's Next Outsourcing Hub: Kenya?" *Christian Science Monitor*, December 21, 2007, http://www.csmonitor.com/2007/1221/p01s02-woaf.html.

ple are left without a bank account and are bypassed altogether by the formal financial sector.

But mobile phones are quickly changing that reality. Entrepreneurs are pioneering a range of mobile banking schemes that provide a growing array of financial services to customers previously without a bank.

Among the most common mobile financial transaction is the innovative use of phone minutes as a tradable commodity—in effect using a virtual currency instead of cash. Mobile subscribers can transfer phone card minutes to another subscriber by sending a text message with a special code. It even has its own language—in Kenya, to send minutes as cash is to "sombassa" someone. The widely popular M-PESA program—M is for mobile, and pesa is Swahili for money—goes further and allows people to deposit money into an account and exchange the deposits for e-money that can be sent to another mobile phone user and redeemed for cash at an M-PESA agent outlet or ATM.

These mobile financial service schemes have many benefits. They bolster the livelihoods of informal workers by allowing them to step beyond cash-denominated transactions. Self-employed entrepreneurs can accept payment on their phones and avoid the security risk of carrying cash. Migrants can send their hard-won income to loved ones hundreds of miles away with a few clicks, saving time and money.

The impact on international remittances is potentially huge. Remittances into Africa exceed a mighty US$8 billion per year, and in some countries like Lesotho and Cape Verde, remittances can reach upwards of 30 percent of GDP.[12] However, traditional remittances have very high transaction costs, often eating up one out of every eight dollars transmitted or more. Operators like Western Union and MoneyGram charge fees as high as US$16 to send US$100.[13] That translates into US$1 billion or more spent just on the transaction costs for remittances to Africa each year. But mobile phones allow people to transfer money for a fraction of the cost. Celtel, one of the largest mobile providers in Africa, now allows customers to transfer money via mobile phones from any bank in the world to banks in Kenya, Tanzania, and Uganda, and to use the phone to manage bank accounts, pay utility bills, transfer cell phone minutes, and use other services, all for a small fraction of the cost of a traditional money transfer.

---

12 Benno Ndulu, "Challenges of African Growth: Opportunities, Constraints, and Strategic Directions" (Washington, D.C.: World Bank, 2007), http://siteresources.worldbank.org/AFRICAEXT/Resources/AFR_Growth_Advance_Edition.pdf.

13 Ratha Dilip, "Leveraging Remittances for Development," Paper presented at the Second Plenary Meeting of the Leading Group on Solidarity Levies to Fund Development, Oslo, February 6–7, 2007, http://siteresources.worldbank.org/INTPROSPECTS/Resources/334934-1110315015165/LeveragingRemittancesForDevelopment.pdf.

In the future, of course, an even broader array of financial services beyond payment and money transfers will be offered to mobile subscribers. In particular, banks and microfinance institutions could reach new customers with credit, savings, and insurance products through the launch of new mobile programs. In fact, this is already beginning to occur. MTN MobileMoney began in South Africa in 2005, initially concentrating on providing basic banking services such as money transfers and account monitoring in conjunction with South Africa's Standard Bank. Mobile-Money replaced physical banks and only required a phone call and government identification to subscribe, helping to bring in rural users and those without bank accounts. But as MobileMoney has evolved, options have increased from the use of an associated credit card to the addition of two other South African banks and numerous alternate payment points at local shops and stores as well as expanded financial services and security options. The program is now being adopted in Uganda and is being tested in five additional pilot programs across Africa, including one in Liberia.

The wide reach of mobile banking has begun to weaken urban and gender biases that traditional banking structures frequently perpetuate. Mobile phone network coverage opens these services to people in the most remote areas who are often ignored by their capitals. Women gain access to markets and services as they begin to use mobile banking individually to manage funds and transactions apart from husbands or collectives. Moreover, mobile banking enhances security for women and youth because, unlike traditional finance, it does not require travel that wastes time, costs money, and exposes vulnerable populations to physical harm. Economically empowering marginalized groups helps level the financial playing field and acts as a democratizing force for economic growth.

Strengthening Health Services Delivery

ICT is already having a big impact on public health and health services delivery. Mobile technology is supporting both prevention and treatment as it allows health officials and providers to disseminate information more quickly and monitor patients more effectively. Public health officials dispatch SMS texts offering information on HIV/AIDS to a sprawling population, effectively reaching and educating a group of people in minutes as opposed to months. For researchers and technicians, mobile technology is providing a faster way to collect health data and to disseminate information quickly and accurately.

Mobile technology has also revolutionized medical treatment and evaluation. SMS texts can remind patients to get their vaccinations or take their TB medicine, or even have relatives remind patients to take the correct dosage of antiretroviral drugs each day. The ability to monitor and remind patients has far-reaching effects. Rwanda is now using text messages to track HIV/AIDS patients in 75 percent of the country's health clinics, allowing the health system to follow up with and track patients, even if they change clinics. And a phone-based system called mPedigree in Ghana is being used to tackle the problem of counterfeit drugs: a scratch-off panel on the packaging reveals a special code that can be texted to verify the drugs' authenticity.[14]

Doctors and nurses are now able to improve health services in understaffed or remote health clinics by performing diagnostics virtually. A rural doctor with scant resources can now use a cell phone to send images of blood smears, eye problems, or skin diseases for diagnosis in the nearest urban hospital or at a clinic on a different continent. Public health officials can even monitor medical inventories throughout a country via text messages. South Africa has deployed an innovative pill bottle equipped with mobile technology, called Simpill, to encourage TB patients to adhere to their medication regiment. When a patient opens the pill bottle, an SMS is sent to a server that stores the data. If the Simpill bottle is not opened on schedule, a reminder SMS can be sent to the patient or to family members.

Strengthening Democracy and Governance

The effects of ICT go far beyond economics and finance. The ability to transmit information quickly to wide audiences has potentially major implications for democracy and governance. For example, mobile technology has played an increasingly important role in helping to constitute freer and fairer elections throughout Africa. Citizens have been given a weapon against corruption and rigged elections, and they are more than willing to use it.

In the 2004 presidential elections in Ghana, for example, voters used their mobile phones to call radio shows to report irregularities, obstruction, and intimidation. Likewise, 500 NGO workers with mobile phones directly monitored the 2007 Sierra Leone elections, sending SMS texts immediately to report irregularities and unofficial vote tallies. In the 2008 Zimbabwean election, supporters of different parties sent SMS text messages with local voting results to help build national tallies. These tech-

---

14 "Beyond Voice: New Uses for Mobile Phones Could Launch Another Wave of Development," Mobile Marvels: A Special Report on Telecoms in Emerging Markets, *The Economist,* September 26, 2009, 10.

nologies are making it much more difficult for those who want to stuff ballot boxes, lose ballots, close polling places, or otherwise thwart the voting process.

Beyond elections, human rights abuses and criminal activity are more easily relayed across a country, and indeed the world, as SMS texts and phone calls pluck an injustice done in a rural area out of obscurity and onto the national stage. Azur Development launched an SMS campaign in the Democratic Republic of the Congo to invite women to report domestic violence. These portrayals were then discussed on a radio show. Mobile technology gives voice to people across great geographic and ideological differences. And it helps deepen public debate on key issues by making it much easier for people to call into radio talk shows. Mo Ibrahim, the Sudanese founder of both Celtel and a foundation to improve governance and transparency, puts it this way: "Mobile phones play a really wonderful role in enabling civil society. As well as empowering people economically and socially, they are a wonderful political tool."[15]

There are, of course, downsides as well. Mobile technology and the Internet can be used to send false information, sometimes on purpose to defame people, or to whip up hostilities against certain groups, as was the case during the 2007 Kenyan elections. These problems are not trivial. They have been an issue for other forms of media and communication over the years, including in newspapers, magazine, radio, television, and landline telephones. In some ways the problems are accelerated by the very speed at which information can flow over ICT channels. But overall the net impact of this greater information and transparency has been positive. And ICT technology can also counter these effects. In Kenya, a website called Ushahidi (which means testimony in Swahili) was established in the aftermath of the elections to map reports of violence. It has since been expanded to several other countries to report human rights violations and provide information for crisis management.

NGO and watchdog groups can post information on government activities, including financial accounts and payments. More governments are posting budget outcomes, audits, and the results of competitive bidding processes online for public scrutiny. The Extractive Industries Transparency Initiative and Publish What You Pay both use information technology to allow for much greater public scrutiny of contracts and payments associated with natural resource industries.

ICT has also enabled some governments to start doing smarter, more efficient business. The ability to enact "e-government" transactions is

---

15 "Eureka Moments: How a Luxury Tool Became a Tool of Global Development," Mobile Marvels. A Special Report on Telecoms in Emerging Markets, *The Economist*, September 26, 2009, 2.

slicing through bureaucracy by reducing the time and cost of transactions, allowing governments to carry out business at a fraction of the previous cost. For example, to foster trade and increase customs revenues, Ghana introduced the GCNet customs system in 2003. The system acts as a one-stop interface, linking all the main players in the clearing process, enabling quick online processing of customs clearance documentation, and facilitating the clearance of goods through ports. The system allows documents and requests to be submitted at any time and allows for round-the-clock verification and monitoring. GCNet increased customs revenues by 49 percent in its first 18 months of operation and reduced clearance times from three weeks to two days

Looking Ahead

Throughout history, new technologies have unleashed transformative social and economic changes. Railroads revolutionized the United States, the Green Revolution transformed agriculture in Asia, the telegraph and the telephone connected people around the globe, and life-saving vaccine technologies have profoundly improved human welfare. Mobile phones, the Internet, and their successors are on their way to having a similar impact across Africa; they already have brought remarkable change and transformation in just a few years. While their effects will go well beyond the emerging countries, the more open political climate and stronger economic policies in these countries create an environment where the impacts of these new technologies are likely to be particularly significant.

Mobile phones and Internet connections are creating new economic opportunities for big businesses and small entrepreneurs alike. New jobs are sprouting up, and old jobs are increasing their profits and incomes. Farmers, market women, taxi drivers, and street hawkers are all reaping the benefits. Increased cash flows from new jobs and easier remittances have made more money available for individuals and families for food, medicines, and school fees. Information is flowing more quickly and easily, helping improve transparency and accountability and adding new citizen voices to maturing democracies.

The implications for the future are huge. These technologies are helping everyday Africans overcome some of the daunting constraints that have inhibited economic growth and poverty reduction in the past, including geographic isolation, weak infrastructure, poor information, and inefficient markets. To be sure, they are not a silver bullet. They will not overcome all problems, lift everyone out of poverty, or change autocratic governments into liberal democracies. But they are surely helping move many countries in Africa in a new direction. They are creating completely new opportunities and options that simply did not exist even 10 years ago, much less 20 years ago during the depths of Africa's economic crisis.

The most exciting part is that they have only just begun to have an impact and are nowhere close to reaching their potential. In the years to come, these technologies and their successors will help lower business costs, create new income opportunities that we cannot now conceive, and help citizens hold their leaders more accountable. They will be a powerful force in helping Africa's emerging countries build on their recent success and continue robust growth, improved governance, and poverty reduction in the future.

7

THE COMING OF THE
"CHEETAHS"

Patrick Awuah knows that Africa's future lies in the education of a new generation of leaders. Born in Ghana, Awuah went to the United States as a teenager to attend Swarthmore College. When Awuah returned to Ghana five years later, he was dismayed by what he saw: an autocratic government, economic ruin, and complete lack of basic services. This was certainly no place to stay and have a career.[1]

Awuah returned to the United States, where he landed a position as a program manager at Microsoft and began to cultivate a successful career and start a family. However, with the birth of his first child, Awuah's perspective on his future—and on the potential for Ghana—began to change. As he says, "Being a parent got me to thinking about a lot of things . . . in particular what effect Africa would have on my children. If that continent can turn around, it will make a big difference in how the world perceives my children because they are African."[2]

Awuah made his choice. He returned to Ghana in 2001 and cofounded Ashesi University, a small liberal arts college that expressly aims to educate Africa's next generation of leaders. As Awuah sees it, Africa's future depends directly on what the new generation of young people does with it. He believes that the question of transformation in Africa is entirely a question of leadership: "Africa can only be transformed by enlightened leaders. Leaders have to be trained and educated right . . . and they are not. There is very little emphasis on ethics [in education] and a stronger

Opposite:

Treating malaria in Iringa, Tanzania (©2010 Mikkel Ostergaard / Panos)

Thanks to Casey Dunning for helping to draft this chapter.

1 Brad Broberg, "Patrick Awuah Left Microsoft to Found Ashesi University," *Puget Sound Business Journal,* September 10, 2004, http://seattle.bizjournals.com/seattle/stories/2004/09/13/focus19.html.

2 Ibid.

sense of entitlement than responsibility so I decided to engage this particular problem."[3]

Ashesi's liberal arts coursework focuses on creating students who are "ethical, entrepreneurial leaders of exceptional integrity with the ability to confront difficult problems and come up with the right solutions."[4] By being intentional about the kind of students and future leaders Ashesi produces, Awuah hopes to create dynamic professionals who are prepared to succeed in all facets of life, from business to politics. As he sees it, a great society can emerge within one generation.

Patrick Awuah and the students of Ashesi University represent a new generation of African leaders—people determined to revolutionize governments, institutions, and communities through innovative thinking, wise leadership, and hard work, rather than through connections, corruption, and force.

The best news is that Patrick is not alone. Throughout Africa, and especially in the emerging countries, a new generation of leaders and entrepreneurs is rising to the top of government bureaucracies, civil society organizations, and businesses. They have been given many labels: "Africa's new hope," "Africa Two," and, most aptly, from Ghanaian scholar George Ayittey, "the Cheetah generation."[5] They have begun quietly and quickly to move into Africa's government bureaucracies, political leadership, private sector, and civil society groups, replacing staid practices with innovation and accountability. They are Africa's new generation, a nebulous yet palpable group across the continent that is seeking to redefine Africa through democracy, transparency, and a dynamic private sector, and by fostering strong connections with each other and with the rest of the world.

They are not defined by age, gender, education, or location. Although most are young, some are older but sick of the old ways of doing things. There are both men and women. Many are well educated, but some come with just street smarts, an idea, and some energy. Most live in urban areas, but they can be found in small villages and towns across the continent running small businesses or local NGOs. What sets them apart is their commitment and their drive to break from the past and move their countries in a new direction.

Ayittey vividly described a "new generation of young Africans who look at African issues and problems from a totally unique perspective. [They

---

3 TED Talk, "Patrick Awuah on Educating Leaders," TED, http://www.ted.com/speakers/patrick_awuah.html.

4 Ibid.

5 George Ayittey, *Africa Unchained: The Blueprint for Africa's Future* (New York: Palgrave Macmillan, 2006).

are] the cheetah generation. They do not relate to the old colonialist paradigm, the slave trade, nor Africa's post-colonialist nationalist leaders."[6] In contrast to the old, slow-moving "hippo" generation, which Ayittey sees as stuck in the past complaining about colonialism and imperialism, this emerging class of entrepreneurs and leaders is focused on transparency, accountability, good governance, respect for basic human rights, and private sector economic opportunities. They are working to position Africa as uniquely Africa, neither tied to nationalist pedagogy nor bound to Western mandates.

Many of Africa's first group of postcolonial presidents and prime ministers rose to power directly from leadership positions in independence movements or rebel armies. Unfortunately, in most cases, they proved to be far more adept at fighting against the colonial government than they were at running their own. Many of those leaders consolidated power in their own hands, weakened mechanisms for accountability and transparency, and hung on in office for far too long (and a few continue to do so). And they installed cronies throughout the government and beyond whose major qualification was loyalty, not competence or accountability. This pattern is by no means unique to Africa; it has been repeated by the first-generation leaders of many newly independent countries around the world. But as Awuah, Ayittey, and many others have argued, these leadership problems were are the heart of Africa's conflict and stagnation.

The old leaders and their styles, ideas, policies, fears, and histories are fading away. They are slowly being replaced by a new generation shaped by different experiences and ideas, a generation poised to overcome some of the most trenchant problems of the past and build a new future for Africa. The new generation wants to end the perception of African countries as basket cases and to present instead stable, safe, and dynamic communities that are productive and responsible members of the international community.

This generational change is now widely noted, both at home and abroad. President Barack Obama pointed to "the young people—brimming with talent and energy and hope . . . speaking up against patronage and participating in the political process" in his first speech in sub-Saharan Africa—fittingly in Accra.[7] Rock star Bono cited the "members of the growing African middle class, who are fed up with being patronized and hearing the song of their majestic continent in a minor key."[8] Many formerly expatriate Africans are returning to their home countries, and

---

6 Ibid, xix.

7 Barack Obama, "Remarks to the Ghanaian Parliament," July 11, 2009. http://www.whitehouse.gov/the_press_office/Remarks-by-the-President-to-the-Ghanaian-Parliament/.

8 Bono, "Rebranding Africa," *New York Times,* July 9, 2009, page A25.

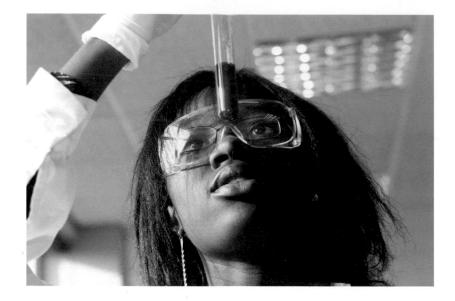

where they have not yet returned, leaders want them back. Liberian President Ellen Johnson Sirleaf—who herself returned after the civil war to lead her country in a fundamentally new direction—called out in her 2006 inaugural address: "We have hundreds of doctors, engineers, and economists, as well as thousands of teachers, nurses, professors, and other Liberians who possess specialized skills currently living abroad. I re-echo my appeal to all of you to please come home! Please make the sacrifice, for your country needs you and needs you now!"[9] Whether returning from abroad to reclaim life in their home country or rising through the system at home, this emerging generation is taking the future into its own hands and moving forward with a new set of standards and strong resolution.

Dr. Agnes Binagwaho heard the call. After she completed her medical training in Belgium and France, Dr. Binagwaho returned to Rwanda in 1996, just after the genocide and as the HIV/AIDS pandemic was beginning to wreak havoc across the continent. "The first week I was back in Rwanda was the worst of my life," she recalled. The drugs to treat HIV/AIDS were too expensive. Women were dying in childbirth for "entirely stupid reasons." "I saw more deaths in one week than I had seen in five years as a pediatrician in France. I nearly packed my bags to go back. There were no resources. Everyone was dying."[10]

Luckily for countless Rwandans, Binagwaho did not leave. For the past 14 years, she has led Rwanda's battle against HIV/AIDS, first as the execu-

9 Ellen Johnson Sirleaf, "Inaugural Address," January 16, 2006, page 4, http://www.emansion.gov.lr/doc/inaugural_add_1.pdf.

10 Christine Gorman, "Anges Binagwaho on Brain Drain," Global Health Report, posted April 23, 2008, http://globalhealthreport.blogspot.com/2008/04/agnes-binagwaho-on-brain-drain.html.

tive secretary of the National Commission for the Fight against HIV/AIDS, and now as the permanent secretary for the Ministry of Health. She has helped develop the standard of care for the treatment of HIV/AIDS patients in Rwanda, improve access to care for communities, and develop the overall national strategy to fight the disease. And with her leadership and the efforts of countless Rwandans, the tide is beginning to turn. The HIV/AIDS adult prevalence rate in Rwanda has fallen steadily from 6 percent in 1997 to under 3 percent today, the number of annual deaths has fallen by 70 percent, and the number of people living with the disease has dropped by one-third.[11] This is what leadership and commitment can do.

But her vision is much bigger. For Binagwaho, confronting HIV/AIDS is just one piece of the economic development puzzle. She is now championing the use of information and communications technologies to improve health care in Rwanda and in the process give people more and better access to information. With a new e-Health system, Binagwaho hopes "to create an effective and sustainable health system that will solve the challenges, such as the lack of infrastructure and the shortage of professionals."[12]

The cheetahs can be found in all walks of society across all of Africa. They are a particularly important presence in the emerging countries, where democratic governance and friendlier economic policies allow them to flourish. Many are joining businesses in managerial or analytic positions in financial firms, cell phone companies, manufacturers, trading houses, and hotels. Others are starting their own businesses, often overcoming long odds to work in the informal sector, using mobile technology to help farmers find data online, introducing mobile cell phone chargers, or opening Internet cafes or small restaurants. They are taking advantage of the more open economic environment with a strong entrepreneurial spirit. They are bringing in new funds for investment, some of it from friends and relatives overseas in the diaspora.

Many combine fresh ideas, entrepreneurship, technology, and just plain energy. Senegal's Amadou Ba is one. He is the cofounder and president of AllAfrica.com, the largest online aggregator and distributor of news from sub-Saharan Africa. AllAfrica.com is affiliated with more than 140 news organizations throughout the continent that feed content into the website. In return, AllAfrica.com markets and shares the various news articles and, importantly, shares the revenues with the various

---

11 UNAIDS, "2008 Report on the Global AIDS Epidemic," UNAIDS, http://www.unaids.org/en/KnowledgeCentre/HIVData/GlobalReport/2008/2008_Global_report.asp.

12 Agnes Binagwaho, "The Use of Information and Communications Technologies (ICT) to Provide and Support Healthcare Service Delivery in Rwanda," Disruptive Women in Health Care, article posted February 4, 2010, http://www.disruptivewomen.net/author/abinagwaho/.

media outlets. Ba also serves as the acting executive director of the African Media Initiative, a program designed to radically change the media landscape in Africa through building capacity and training journalists, media managers, information technology workers, and a host of other media and journalism professionals. Ba wants the African Media Initiative to play a prominent role in the future of African media and help to "strengthen the progress that has been made so far and take the media landscape to the next level." With "patient capital and a holistic approach to investment in the continent," Ba believes that the media space in Africa will become even more far-reaching and robust to support a growing and vibrant Africa.[13]

Others are joining the government. A new generation of capable ministers, deputies, and directors are beginning to play pivotal roles in strengthening policy analysis and making governments more efficient and effective. Many have returned from lucrative jobs abroad to underpaid jobs in their native homes simply to have the chance to effect change for a more promising future.

Amara Konneh fled Liberia when he was 20 years old when his family was viciously gunned down in the civil war. After a long and difficult journey, he made his way to a refugee camp in the remote village of Musardou in Guinea. He watched Liberian refugees in the camp die from hunger, poverty, and disease and decided to do something. He helped form a refugee committee for the camp that took a census and kept birth and death records and used this information to advocate for larger food supplies from the United Nations High Commission on Refugees. He then went to the local chiefs to ask for a piece of land to grow beans and corn, sold the crops on the local market, and used the proceeds to rehabilitate an abandoned building and turn it into a school for children from the camp. He soon had more than 100 students and impressed the International Rescue Committee so much that they began to provide school supplies and pay some of the teachers. They then hired Konneh as the refugee education coordinator for the district.

At age 23, he made his way to the United States, where he worked his way through Delaware County Community College, earned a bachelor's degree from Drexel University, and eventually a graduate degree in Management Information Systems from Penn State. He landed a plum job as a financial systems analyst at the Vanguard Group of Investment Companies and settled down to enjoy life with his wife and children.[14]

---

13 David Sasaki, "Interview with Amadou M. Ba of AllAfrica.com," Rising Voices, article posted October 10, 2009, http://rising.globalvoicesonline.org/blog/2009/10/10/video-interview-with-amadou-m-ba-of-allafrica-com.

14 Amara Konneh, interview with the author, December 15, 2009.

He could have very comfortably stayed put. But when Liberia's civil war ended in 2003 and the presidential elections heated up in 2005, he could not sit back and watch from afar. Although he had never met Ellen Johnson Sirleaf, he took a leave of absence from his job to sign up for her campaign. She was impressed and offered him a job, so following her inauguration he moved back to Liberia. After 18 months in the president's office spearheading information technology initiatives, he went to the Kennedy School of Government at Harvard University to study public administration. He returned in 2008 at age 38 to become the minister of planning, one of the youngest ministers on the continent. He has attracted a smart young staff, and they are moving fast to develop strategies for growth and poverty reduction and to change relationships with donors, NGOs, and others supporting those strategies. Konneh typifies the cheetah generation: young, energetic, technically savvy, and shaped by experiences both at home and around the world. They are poised to lead the emerging countries to a future very different from the past.

They are also poised to change the gender biases of the past. Women are moving into higher-profile private and public positions, as they become income earners, civil society leaders, political leaders, and government officials. Shifting gender paradigms have played a crucial role in defining the cheetah generation; an increased focus on women and girls has created the opportunity for women to enter into traditionally "masculine" roles and jobs. The education and professionalization of women adds a whole new dimension to the available skilled workforce, doubling Africa's human capital potential.

Kenya's Wangari Maathai was a great leader in the spirit of the cheetah generation long before most of the new generation was even born. A scientist by training, she has always been a trailblazer. She was the first woman in East Africa to earn a doctorate degree, and she became chair of the Department of Veterinary Anatomy at the University of Nairobi in 1976. During the late 1970s and early 1980s, she rose to leadership positions in several key civic organizations, including director of the Kenyan Red Cross Society, chair of the board of the Environment Liaison Center, and chair of the National Council of Women in Kenya. In 1977, she founded what eventually became the Green Belt Movement, a broad-based grassroots organization dedicated to organizing groups of women to plant trees to preserve the environment, create jobs, and improve the quality of life. The Green Belt Movement has helped women plant more than 20 million trees on their farms, school grounds, and church compounds. In 1986, the movement established a Pan African Green Belt Movement, and started chapters in

Tanzania, Uganda, Malawi, Lesotho, Ethiopia, Zimbabwe, and several other countries.

Maathai's work with the Green Belt Movement and her growing calls for democracy brought her into repeated conflicts with the government of Daniel Arap Moi during the late 1980s and 1990s. She led a number of protests, regularly spoke out against the government on both democracy and environmental issues, and was briefly jailed on several occasions. She became a leader of the growing democracy movement, ran for parliament several times, and finally won a seat in the 2002 election that brought an end to Moi's 24-year reign. In January 2003, she was appointed assistant minister of environment and natural resources. In 2004, she was awarded the Nobel Peace Prize in recognition of her efforts, the first African woman and environmentalist to win the honor. Wangari Maathai is proof of the changes that can come from one woman's energy, ideas, and determination.[15]

Some of the cheetahs made major contributions first at home, and now are contributing to Africa's revival as leaders in international organizations. Ngozi Okonjo-Iweala, Nigeria's first female minister of finance, tirelessly led the fight against corruption in her home country and was later appointed managing director of the World Bank in 2007. Antoinette Sayeh served as Liberia's minister of finance following the election of Ellen Johnson Sirleaf, and is now director of the Africa Department of the International Monetary Fund. And the best known of all is Kofi Annan, who served as the secretary-general of the United Nations from 1997 through 2006 and was a co-recipient (with the UN) of the 2001 Nobel Peace Prize.

Many have played changing roles over time. Benno Ndulu is a leading thinker about economic development in Africa, an accomplished teacher, and a prominent policymaker. Ndulu was the lead author of the African Economic Research Consortium (AERC) study on economic growth in Africa that I have referred to many times in this book. His extensive writing has been a major force in shaping the debate and thinking on economic development in Africa. But he has been more than a writer. Ndulu was instrumental in setting up the AERC in 1988, and served as its first research director and later as its executive director. The AERC's Collaborative Masters Degree Program, based at African universities with a joint faculty at AERC in Nairobi, has graduated more than 1,700 well-trained master's students in economics between its founding in 1993 and 2009. Its collaborative PhD program has produced 58 PhDs since 2000.

---

15 This account is drawn from Wangari Maathai's autobiography, *Unbowed: A Memoir* (New York: Knopf Publishing Group, 2006).

These graduates are making a difference in public and private sector positions throughout SSA.[16] In 2008, Ndulu became the governor of the Central Bank of Tanzania, where he is shaping economic policy and laying the foundation for Tanzania's continued economic success.

The cheetahs outside of emerging Africa are beginning to provide hope as well; given the chance, they will be central to igniting change in their own countries. Doing so will take dogged determination, and nobody exemplifies this better than Zimbabwe's Tererai Trent. *New York Times* columnist Nick Kristof tells the amazing story of this village cattle herder turned PhD:

> Tererai was born in a village in rural Zimbabwe . . . and attended elementary school for less than one year. Her father married her off when she was about 11 to a man who beat her regularly. She seemed destined to be one more squandered African asset. A dozen years passed. Jo Luck, the head of an aid group called Heifer International, passed through the village and told the women there that they should stand up, nurture dreams, change their lives. Inspired, Tererai scribbled down four absurd goals. . . . She wrote that she wanted to study abroad, and to earn a BA, a master's, and a doctorate.
>
> Tererai began to work for Heifer and several Christian organizations as a community organizer. She used the income to take correspondence courses, while saving every penny she could. In 1998 she was accepted to Oklahoma State University, but she insisted on taking all five of her children with her rather than leave them with her husband. "I couldn't abandon my kids," she recalled. "I knew that they might end up getting married off." Tererai's husband eventually agreed that she could take the children to America—as long as he went too. Heifer helped with the plane tickets, Tererai's mother sold a cow, and neighbors sold goats to help raise money. With US$4,000 in cash wrapped in a stocking and tied around her waist, Tererai set off for Oklahoma.
>
> An impossible dream had come true, but it soon looked like a nightmare. Tererai and her family had little money and lived in a ramshackle trailer, shivering and hungry. Her husband refused to do any housework he was a man!—and coped by beating her. "There was very little food," she said. "The kids would come home from school, and they would be hungry." Tererai found herself eating from trash cans, and she thought about quitting—but felt that doing so would let down other African women.
>
> "I knew that I was getting an opportunity that other women were dying to get," she recalled. So she struggled on, holding several jobs, taking every class she could, washing and scrubbing, enduring beatings, barely sleeping. At one point the university tried to expel Tererai for falling behind on tuition payments. A university official, Ron Beer, intervened on her behalf and rallied the faculty and community behind her with donations and support.

---

16 Thanks to Steve O'Connell for the background information on the AERC degree programs.

"I saw that she had enormous talent," Dr. Beer said. His church helped with food, Habitat for Humanity provided housing, and a friend at Wal-Mart carefully put expired fruits and vegetables in boxes beside the dumpster and tipped her off.

Soon afterward, Tererai had her husband deported back to Zimbabwe for beating her, and she earned her BA—and started on her MA. Then her husband returned, now frail and sick with a disease that turned out to be AIDS. Tererai tested negative for HIV, and then, feeling sorry for her husband, she took in her former tormentor and nursed him as he grew sicker and eventually died.

Through all this blur of pressures, Tererai excelled at school, pursuing a PhD at Western Michigan University and writing a dissertation on AIDS prevention in Africa even as she began working for Heifer as a program evaluator.[17]

Tererai Trent, now Dr. Tererai Trent, completed her PhD in December 2009. When she gets the chance, there is little doubt she will be a major force for change in Zimbabwe.

The cheetah generation means many things, but five stand out: ideas, technology, entrepreneurship, market power, and the push for good governance and accountability. First, they are bringing fresh ideas to the table in business, government, and civil society. As Ayittey has pointed out, they do not see the world through the lens of colonialism, imperialism, socialism, or the Cold War. They are self-reliant and self-starters. They are providing new thinking and perspectives on brand new businesses, such as biomass fuel for cleaner and smaller-scale energy in rural areas, and on how to organize old businesses better, including everything from bakeries to breweries. They come with ideas and strategies for organizing communities, particularly youth, to provide local services and speak out in political debates. And they come with ideas and approaches for using the private sector to solve what were once seen as public sector problems, such as supplying clean water and basic health services.

William Kamkwamba is full of ideas. The young Malawian began inventing when he was just 14 years old, after he had to drop out of school when his family could no longer afford his tuition. He built his family an electricity-generating windmill using blue gum trees, bicycle parts, and materials collected in a local scrap yard, and working from rough plans he found in a library book. His description illustrates great entrepreneurial spirit:

After I dropped out from school, I went to the library, and I read a book that was called *Using Energy,* and I got information about doing the mill. And I tried and I made it. In fact, the design of the windmill that was in the book,

17 Nicholas Kristoff, "Triumph of a Dreamer," *New York Times,* November 14, 2009, http://www.nytimes.com/2009/11/15/opinion/15kristof.html.

it had three blades, and I made four blades because I wanted to increase power. I used a bicycle frame, and a pulley, and plastic pipe, and it produced 12 watts—enough to power four bulbs and two radios.[18]

Since then, he has built a solar-powered water pump that supplies the first drinking water in his village of Wimbe and two other windmills (the tallest standing at 39 feet), and he is planning two more.[19] His work inspired the founding of the Moving Windmills Project, which works with local leaders to design, organize, and implement appropriate solutions for problems in food, clothing, shelter, sanitation, health, education, clean water, and community building. William's latest project is to team with Moving Windmills and buildOn.org to rebuild the Wimbe Primary School. William's energy and ideas are solving problems and helping to bring electricity, water, and education to the people of Wimbe.

Second, the cheetahs are at the forefront of introducing innovative technologies that are creating new opportunities and solving old problems. In the last chapter we explored these new technologies, especially mobile phones and the Internet. But just as important as the technologies themselves are the people who are bringing them. New technologies would not have had the same impact if it were not for the people who understand them and have the creativity to figure out how to use them. Young Africans who have lived in Europe or the United States are deeply comfortable with new technologies and with adapting quickly to even newer ones. And having experienced the wide-ranging applications of these technologies elsewhere, they have the capacity and vision to bring them home and apply them to new problems. Whether it is creating the platform for farmers to get crop prices, figuring out how to transfer money more safely and easily or how to transfer health data to rural nurses, or establishing a mechanism for more open political debate, the cheetahs are at the cutting edge of making these new technologies work. It takes both the technology and the cheetahs to make it happen.

Third, the cheetahs bring a new entrepreneurial energy to business enterprises, small and large. The cheetahs are both taking advantage of the economic opening in the emerging countries and pushing hard to further reduce barriers against business. They include young farmers introducing sesame seeds to sell to market, investment bankers working out of Johannesburg, tailors opening a second (or third) clothing shop, cell phone operators selling minutes back in their villages, engineers de-

---

18 Transcript from "William Kamkwamba on Building a Windmill," TED Global 2007, http://www.ted.com/talks/william_kamkwamba_on_building_a_windmill.html.

19 Sarah Childress, "A Young Tinkerer Builds a Windmill, Electrifying a Nation," *Wall Street Journal*, December 12, 2007, A1. See also William Kamkwamba and Bryan Mealer, *The Boy Who Harnessed the Wind: Creating Currents of Electricity and Hope* (London: William Morrow, 2009).

veloping new ideas for solar power, and horticulturists selling cut flowers from Uganda and Kenya. The cheetahs share the energy, determination, and self-reliance to make their businesses of all sizes work.

Masetumo Lebitsa knows how to overcome the odds. When the European women who had started Lesotho's mohair weaving industry
abruptly left in the early 1990s because of the political turmoil sur-
rounding the end of apartheid in neighboring South Africa, the local
weavers were left to fend for themselves. With little education and less
business management training, these women faced an uphill battle trying to operate successful businesses. Many failed. But not Lebitsa. She
organized the women that remained in a small company called Matela
Weavers, formed an association, and changed the name to Maseru Tapestries and Mats. She signed up for free artisan training programs to
develop her business skills. She interviewed her clients to get a better
idea of what they wanted and needed, in effect performing her own
marketing survey. And she kept at it. Despite a number of initial difficult
years, Lebitsa was focused on succeeding on her own merits, noting "I
want to have my business run like a real business. I don't want to continue to take handouts." Lebitsa has built Maseru Tapestries and Mats
into a thriving business, taking orders from visitors, diplomats, and even

the king. Her business has gone international, and her weavings are now sold in Southern Africa, Europe, and the United States.[20]

Fourth, the cheetahs are a powerful consumer force. They are not just starting their own businesses, as important as that is. With their size and buying power they are the customer base for a wide range of goods and services: banking, mobile phones, restaurants, theaters, bookstores, coffee shops, tailors, and a range of other consumer goods.[21] Some cheetahs are investing in businesses specifically designed to cater to other cheetahs. For investors, they are a growing force that cannot be ignored.

Fifth, the cheetahs are leading the charge for greater transparency, accountability, and honesty. Partly because of their ingrained use of technology and their globalized outlook, they expect open debate, tolerance for opposition, and much better data and information on what is happening. They expect governments to post information quickly on key government policies and financial information, including budget outcomes, contracts with investors, major policy decisions, and pending legislation. They do not easily tolerate delays or hiding of information. For many, the question is not whether democracy makes sense—that seems patently obvious—but how to make it work better and hold elected leaders more accountable for their actions. And they carry a lot of votes; the young generation makes up a huge and growing portion of the populations of the emerging countries, gaining increasing power to choose their leaders.

Sometimes being a cheetah comes at a price, especially for those fighting against corruption. Kenya's John Githongo is a former journalist who at age 34 founded and subsequently ran the Kenyan chapter of Transparency International, an NGO devoted to transparency, accountability, and good governance. Four years later, newly elected Kenyan President Mwai Kibaki, who had run on an anticorruption platform following the 24-year reign of Daniel arap Moi, appointed Githongo as permanent secretary for governance and ethics in the president's office. He had two tasks: investigate corruption perpetrated under Moi and take steps to prevent new government officials from following the same path.

He was making good progress on both counts, but apparently making too much progress on the second to suit the tastes of some of his new colleagues. After just two years he abruptly fled to London and resigned. The

---

20 Masetumo Lebitsa, e-mail interview, May 6, 2010. See also "Maseru Tapestries and Mats," AfricanCrafts.com, http://www.africancrafts.com/artisan.php?sid=32937883115182448238975381169031&id=maseru&pg=intro.

21 See Vijay Mahajan, *Africa Rising: How 900 Million African Consumers Offer More Than You Think* (Philadelphia: Wharton School Publishing, 2008).

Surveying an open-pit copper mine in Zambia

reason became clear only later: he had uncovered a series of corrupt procurement deals involving several senior government officials worth hundreds of millions of dollars, and his life was under serious threat. He could have decided to stay and remain silent. After all, he belonged to the elite, was raised in comfort, was close to the president, and could have expected a long and financially rewarding career had he played along. But his conscience wouldn't let him. Since 2004, he has lived in exile in London, teaching, writing, speaking, and doing all he can to keep pushing for good governance back home. But chances are that at some point in the future, Githongo will have his chance to return home.

In many ways Githongo epitomizes the courage of the cheetah generation. Michela Wrong, the author of a biography about Githongo, put it this way: "I am convinced that the Githongo story is one of those flares that history periodically sends up, alerting us to an important change taking place on the continent: a generation of well-educated, self-confident, and frustrated young Africans is preparing to call time on its fathers' ways of doing business."[22]

✳ ✳ ✳

This book has analyzed some of the key transformations that are taking place across the emerging countries: the shift to democracy, the introduction of more sensible economic policies, the end of the debt crisis, the establishment of better relationships with the international community, and the rise of new technologies. The cheetahs are a bit different from these other transformations; they are not so much a thing that is changing as they are the driving force that is bringing about that change. They are the force that brings together these other changes, gives them their power, and brings them to life.

The cheetahs are pushing hard for more representational and democratic governments and demanding transparency and accountability.

22 See Michela Wrong, "NS Profile—John Githongo," *New Statesman*, February 6, 2006, http://www. newstatesman.com/200602060018; Michela Wrong, "The Buck Stops Here," *Financial Times*, January 19, 2007, http://www.ft.com/cms/s/2/1c4e2482-a6c0-11db-83e4-0000779e2340.html; and Michela Wrong, *It's Our Turn to Eat: The Story of a Kenyan Whistleblower* (London: Fourth Estate, 2009).

They are willing to stand up, be heard, and push back against the old ways of doing business. They are strong advocates for a better business environment, less red tape, and more space for small business and entrepreneurs. They have little time for talk of strong forms of socialism and heavy state intervention. They are demanding their voices be heard in discussions and debates about their countries' poverty reduction strategies and in negotiations with donors, sometimes pushing back on their governments' old ways of thinking, and sometimes pushing back on donors when they are stuck in their bureaucratic and paternalistic mindsets. And they are the main vehicles for introducing new technologies to solve long-standing problems in imaginative ways.

All of this bodes well for sustaining the progress of the emerging countries. The cheetahs are coming to the fore as the new generation of talented leaders in business, government, politics, and civil society. The future is in their hands. And in their hands the future looks bright.

CHALLENGES and **OPPORTUNITIES** on the ROAD AHEAD

Africa's emerging countries are on the move. The 300 million people in these 17 countries have put behind them the years of conflict, stagnation, mismanagement, and poor governance. They are moving in a new direction. Economic growth has accelerated, investment is growing, and trade is expanding. Average incomes have increased by 50 percent in just 15 years. Infant mortality rates are down and primary school enrollment is up, especially for girls. Poverty rates have fallen from 59 percent to 48 percent. Democracy, imperfect as it may be, has become the norm rather than the exception. Governance has slowly but steadily improved.

As we have seen, this break from the past stems from several deep and fundamental transformations that are under way in the emerging countries. The dramatic shift toward democracy has brought more capable leadership, greater accountability, and better governance. Stronger economic policies—much less state intervention, fewer disincentives and penalties against agriculture, and a healthier business climate—have encouraged new investment, unleashed entrepreneurial energy, and sparked economic growth. Three other major changes have helped sustain and accelerate progress in recent years. The end of the 25-year debt crisis has freed up financial resources, created more space for well-governed countries to design their own strategies for sustained development and poverty reduction, and changed how donors support these countries. The rapid spread of cell phones and the Internet have helped diminish geographical barriers, created a wide range of new economic opportunities, and introduced new mechanisms for transparency and political accountability. And a new generation of political, business, and community leaders is rising to the fore, bringing new ideas and energy to lead the emerging countries into the future.

Collectively, these five changes form the basis for optimism for the future of the emerging countries. They provide the foundation for strengthening accountability and good governance, expanding economic opportunities and prosperity, fighting disease and illiteracy, and reducing poverty. And they provide models, and hope, for other countries in SSA and elsewhere that are struggling to escape stagnation and poverty.

The emerging countries are not perfect. It's easy for pessimists to point to a litany of flaws, including sometimes deficient elections, continued corruption, weak government capacity, extensive red tape, and insufficient progress in fighting rural poverty. But the change is clear. We should not hold these countries to impossibly high standards and expect that all problems can be solved overnight. Their significant progress should not be dismissed just because it has not yet gone far enough, or because some of their neighbors have not yet started along this road.

Still, while there are strong grounds for optimism, it should be guarded optimism. The economic and political renaissance in these countries is in its early stages and remains fragile. Their continued success is hardly assured. Most of the emerging countries are still very poor, with weak institutions, significant capacity constraints, and limited financial resources. While the shift to democracy has been dramatic, it is still a work in progress. And although there is growing momentum for progress, there continue to be forces within each country—weaker than before, but still evident—that push against further reform, preferring systems of a small elite with strong, unaccountable control of political power and economic resources. And there are several major global forces that could create difficulties in the future.

Challenges Ahead

Looking forward, the emerging countries face several key challenges that will determine the extent to which they can continue their recent success. Five stand out.

1. **Deepening democracy and strengthening governance.**

The transformation from authoritarian rule to more democratic and accountable governments in SSA since 1989 is remarkable, all the more so because so many of the new democracies are poor. Never before in history have so many poor countries shifted to democracy in so short a time. And alongside the shift to democracy has been an evolution toward stronger and more accountable governance. Although not all of the emerging countries are democracies, most are, and even the nondemocracies have taken some initial first steps toward increased accountability and better governance.

In other parts of the world, especially Asia, some authoritarian governments have successfully promoted development, sparking a long-running debate about the relationship between democracy and economic performance.[1] But in Africa the relationship is clear. Authoritarian governments in Africa have been development disasters. By contrast, the strongest democracies have had the best and most sustained economic performance, starting with Botswana and Mauritius and extending today to South Africa, Ghana, Cape Verde, Lesotho, Mozambique, and several others.

Still, while there has been significant progress, the democratic transition in SSA is far from complete. The institutions, attitudes, and cultural norms that undergird democracy require generations to take firm root. Thus, a major challenge for the emerging countries will be to continue to deepen their nascent democratic institutions and further strengthen governance.[2]

This issue is absolutely central to everything else: only through stronger and more accountable democratic governments will the emerging countries be able to continue to strengthen economic management, attract investment, expand the reach of new technologies, open more opportunities for women and ethnic minorities, improve health and education services, and improve and maintain the prosperity of their citizens.

The core issues for further strengthening democratic governance are not concerned so much with elections—which get all the attention—as with strengthening checks and balances on power: more effective legislative and judicial branches and increased transparency, accountability, and citizen voice. Most of the focus in Africa's emerging democracies in the past 20 years has been on the executive branch, and for good reason, given the ruinous record of the authoritarian regimes of the past. But going forward, it will be imperative to strengthen the capacity and operations of both the legislative and judicial branches of power as well.

Strong legislatures are central to mature democracies because they represent a society's diverse interests and provide a degree of oversight

---

1 Morton Halperin, Joseph Siegle, and Michael Weinstein make the case that, despite the strong economic performance of some authoritarian governments, overall democracies have been more successful economically over time than nondemocracies. See Morton Halperin, Joseph Siegle, and Michael Weinstein, *The Democracy Advantage: How Democracies Promote Prosperity and Peace* (New York: Routledge, 2010).

2 For an excellent exposition on the issues of sustaining emerging democracies, see Ethan Kapstein and Nathan Converse, *The Fate of Young Democracies* (Cambridge: Cambridge University Press, 2008).

of government institutions. But, as political scientist Joel Barkan has pointed out, legislatures in Africa have remained relatively weak, even as so many countries have moved to democracy.[3] This is a typical pattern; legislatures rarely begin to play a significant role until after the second or third cycle of multiparty elections, a stage that SSA's emerging democracies are just now entering. African legislatures can be further strengthened as important forces for representation and accountability by improving basic pay to attract competent and honest people, changing rules and procedures to balance power better across the branches of government, building committee systems, establishing budget offices, and professionalizing the legislative staff. A similar set of processes will be required to strengthen judicial and legal systems. Look for these kinds of changes to take shape as Africa's emerging democracies begin to mature.

In addition, transparency and open flows of information are critical checks on power. Accountable governments must be willing to be transparent about their actions and to publicly publish key policy decisions, contracts, budget outcomes, and audit results. A free press is central, especially radio, but also television, newspapers, the Internet, and other outlets for debate. Allowing and encouraging open discourse and dissent, even when the quality and accuracy of the reporting and blogging is weak, is at the core of making governments more responsible. Working across countries, the African Union's New Partnership for Africa's Development (NEPAD) and its African Peer Review Mechanism are potentially powerful vehicles for governments in the region to hold each other accountable and to improve governance further.

Transparency around natural resource contracts is a particularly important issue for the emerging countries, as natural resource extraction has been at the heart of so much corruption in the past. An excellent model is the Extractive Industries Transparency Initiative (EITI), a global standard for transparency in oil, gas, and mining industries. Under the EITI, countries verify and publish contracts, payments, and revenues in extractives sectors. Liberia became the first African country to become fully compliant with the EITI in 2009 (adding forestry to the list of activities covered), and several other emerging countries are candidate countries. Given both the potential damage from natural resource exports (corruption and the negative impact on other exports through exchange-rate appreciation) and the potential benefits (job creation and revenues), it is crucial for countries to establish transparent and competitive bidding processes for contracts, publish the final contracts,

---

3 For an excellent analysis of the role of legislatures in African democracies, see Joel Barkan, ed., *Legislative Power in Emerging African Democracies* (Boulder, CO: Lynne Rienner, 2009).

and publish all payments, revenues, and expenditures derived from natural resources.[4]

And while governance has improved in the emerging countries, several have not gone far enough in the transition to democracy, in particular Ethiopia, Rwanda, and Uganda. In these countries, ongoing conflict, the concentration of power in the executive, and the lack of clear processes for inevitable leadership transitions are causing concern that economic and good governance gains will be difficult to sustain. For them, the crucial transitions still lie ahead, and they are likely to take time. History makes clear that democratic transitions are not always quick and that they are not always certain. Democracy was a long time coming in South Korea and Indonesia, among others. And in Ghana, which in the late 1990s looked a lot like Uganda today, it took 19 years for Jerry Rawlings to step down for an elected successor and clear the way for today's success. There is no guarantee that Uganda will follow the path of Ghana; it could just as easily slip back into authoritarianism. Until Ethiopia, Uganda, and Rwanda achieve a successful political transition and strengthen their democratic institutions, they face greater risks of reversal, and therefore their futures are uncertain.

2. Creating new economic opportunities for a growing workforce.

Although the emerging countries have experienced a growth renaissance since the mid-1990s, they still rely very heavily on a narrow economic base of raw materials, which, if not expanded to new products, will significantly limit their future growth potential. At the same time, while population growth rates are slowing, there are millions of low-skilled workers joining the workforce each year. These two forces creates a major challenge: in order to sustain growth and create new jobs, the emerging countries must diversify into a much broader range of products that rely (at least to begin with) on low-skilled workers and that can be competitive in local, regional, and global markets. There is a wide range of possibilities, including traditional and new agricultural crops, horticulture, fisheries, food processing, clothing, jewelry, toys, furniture, data entry, call centers, tourism, financial services, and many more. Some investment in these areas is already starting. The challenge is how to get more—much more.

While the diversification argument sounds like nerdy economics, it is crucial. Without more diversified economic opportunities, economic growth and poverty reduction will almost certainly stall eventually. Throughout history around the world, this "structural transformation"

---

4 See also Paul Collier, *The Bottom Billion: Why the Poorest Countries Are Failing and What Can Be Done About It* (New York: Oxford University Press, 2007).

from raw materials into diversified production is the *sine qua non* of sustained economic development. A more diverse economy has many benefits: it reduces vulnerability to commodity shocks, creates new and better-paying jobs, and stimulates the productivity gains that lead to higher wages, higher income, and reduced poverty over time. There is a clear political dimension as well: the best way to solidify continued support for the new direction of the emerging countries is to broaden the base of people who benefit directly from it.

This transformation will be neither easy nor automatic. While the specific actions will differ across countries, for most it will require actions in three key areas: supporting agriculture, reducing business costs (especially for trade), and expanding infrastructure.

The critical starting point is to increase agricultural productivity. Agriculture typically accounts for more than 40 percent of GDP and 60 percent of employment and is the key source of income for the vast majority of the rural poor. A productive agricultural sector is not only the main engine for raising rural incomes; it is also critical to keeping prices low and stable for consumers, and for building the foundation for competitive manufacturing and service activities. Revitalizing agriculture is all the more important because climate change is likely to hit agricultural production hard in SSA, as discussed below. Doing so will require creating strong extension services, building roads to connect farmers to consumers and to improve local and regional market integration, ensuring that price and tariff policies do not penalize farmers, and investing in developing new seed and fertilizer technologies and making them widely available.

At the same time, to broaden the economic base into downstream agro-processing, labor-intensive manufacturing, tourism, and data entry services, and small businesses, governments must continue to improve the business climate so firms can compete in global markets. Ultimately, because of their small size, the emerging economies can continue to expand and diversify only through greater integration in international markets, both global and regional. Greater integration will bring with it new technologies, new ideas, and new opportunities for expansion and prosperity.

Some claim that African businesses can't compete in global markets against firms from China, India, or other countries. It is true that competing in global markets will not be easy. But part of the answer is that there is little choice: given the limited growth potential from domestic markets, the emerging countries can't afford *not* to compete in global markets. The history of trade and development tells us that—with well-designed policies and supporting institutions—trade is not a race to the bottom but the surest ladder to the top. Moreover, the rise of China and India creates opportunities as well as competition, as we discuss below.

But more important, the idea that African firms can't compete is simply outdated, not to mention outright condescending. There are plenty of examples of African firms that have become very successful on global markets in the last 10 years, including Kenya's flower exporters, Mali's mango producers, South Africa's cell phone providers and financial companies, Ghana's data entry firms, Mozambique's aluminum smelter, Lesotho's garment producers, and Rwanda's tourism industry.[5]

Emerging Africa's continuing economic success will depend to a large extent on how well it can attract new investors in these kinds of activities. The challenge is to create an environment where entrepreneurs can flourish, and where they are not penalized by unnecessary barriers and obstacles. There is still too much red tape, too many bureaucratic hurdles, and too many opportunities for bribes, all of which ultimately discourage investors from starting new businesses and eat into the wages of everyday workers. For firms to be competitive and create new jobs, these obstacles and barriers must be removed, and some of the key institutions that support trade (such as customs, port management, and export processing zones) will have to be strengthened.

Perhaps most important, almost all of the emerging countries face major infrastructure deficits in roads, power, ports, and telecommunications. Weak infrastructure undermines market opportunities and raises costs, rendering many firms uncompetitive. Electricity costs are substantially higher in Africa than in other parts of the world. The cost of Internet connectivity also remains very high, limiting a range of new economic opportunities. These costs translate directly into reduced investment and lower wages. It will be very difficult for the emerging countries to continue to diversify production, compete on global markets, sustain economic growth, and reduce poverty in the absence of major infrastructure investments.

3. Managing the rise of China.

China has exploded onto the scene in SSA, influencing trade, investment, foreign assistance, and diplomatic relationships. China's trade with SSA exceeds US$100 billion, and China is likely to soon become Africa's largest trading partner.[6] China's influence across the region is uneven; the

---

5 For more examples, see Vijay Mahajan, *Africa Rising: How 900 Million African Consumers Offer More Than You Think* (Philadelphia: Wharton School Publishing, 2008); World Bank, *Yes Africa Can: Success Stories from a Dynamic Continent*, (Washington, DC: World Bank, 2010), http://go.worldbank.org/UIMS7DOXE0; and David Fick, *Africa: Continent of Economic Opportunity* (Johannesburg: STE Publishers, 2006).

6 Rockefeller Foundation, "China's Engagement in African Countries," A Rockefeller Foundation Exploration (New York: Rockefeller Foundation, 2009), http://www.rockefellerfoundation.org/news/publications/chinas-engagement-african-countries.

bulk of its trade and investment is concentrated in a few countries where it has a large presence, while in others its influence is small. Within the emerging countries, Chinese investment is heavily concentrated in South Africa, Zambia, and a few other countries (Table 8.1). But even excluding these two countries, Chinese investment in the emerging countries *quintupled* to over $100 million in just three years between 2005 and 2008. There is little doubt that the rise of China is one of the most powerful economic forces sweeping across Africa.

China's growing role creates many opportunities and potential benefits. It provides a new market for raw materials and other exports and is a source for low-cost capital and consumer goods. Its demand for raw materials has created new jobs, raised prices for many export products, and brought new investments in agriculture, energy, mining, and telecommunications. China is helping finance much-needed infrastructure projects throughout the continent and is providing valuable assistance in agriculture and other areas.

But China's new role also raises several concerns, and many countries are finding that there are multiple sides to the growing relationship with China. Some worry China will repeat the pattern of European and American investors of the past and extract natural resources with little effort to support diversification into downstream products. Almost all of China's aid is provided as loans, creating concerns about a new round of future debt problems. A major concern is that a lack of transparency in negotiating and implementing agreements might facilitate corruption, undermine good governance, and violate environmental and labor standards, leading to deals that ultimately may do more harm than good. Chinese workers in Africa are seen as displacing African workers, and there are serious charges that Chinese managers mistreat African workers. In 2005, for example, 46 workers died in an accident at the Chinese-owned Chambishi copper mine in Zambia, and several months later the miners rioted over low wages and poor conditions. Zambian resentment of China's growing presence spilled over into riots and looting of Chinese shops following the 2006 presidential elections, after opposition candidate Michael Sata

TABLE 8.1 China's Presence Is Large and Growing, but Concentrated in a Few Countries
Foreign Direct Investment from China (millions of USD)

	2005	2008
Botswana	4	14
Ethiopia	5	10
Ghana	3	11
Lesotho	1	1
Mauritius	2	34
Mozambique	3	6
Namibia	0	8
Rwanda	1	13
South Africa	47	4,808
Uganda	0	-7
Tanzania	1	18
Zambia	10	214
Total	**77**	**5,129**
Total excluding South Africa and Zambia	19	108

Source: United Nations Conference on Trade and Development, FDI Statistics database.

accused China of "exploitation" and turning Zambia into a "dumping ground."[7]

Whether the benefits of China's rise in Africa will ultimately outweigh the risks will be determined by how well governments and leaders in the emerging countries manage the relationship—and make no mistake, it will take active management. The keys will be to insist on openness and transparency, to ensure that investment and aid projects fit into the country's own priorities and strategies, and to make certain that wages and working conditions in Chinese operations are at least as good as in similar investments. It will be important for African governments to say no sometimes. The emerging countries must make sure that Chinese bids for concession agreements are part of fully open and competitive processes, with the agreements made publicly available. They should regularly publish information on compliance with payments and other terms of the agreements. Making Chinese investments—alongside all foreign investments—fully transparent along the lines of the EITI and Publish What You Pay Initiative will go a long way toward making that a reality. And to the extent that projects involve borrowing or guarantees on borrowing, governments must proceed with extra caution and ensure that the new borrowing and contingent liabilities are consistent with long-term debt sustainability.

4. **Adapting to climate change.**

By most estimates, climate change will increase global temperatures by between 2° and 5° Celsius over pre-industrial levels by the end of this century, with potentially profound effects on developing countries, including Africa's emerging countries. Climate change could undermine agricultural productivity, strain water supplies, increase droughts and flooding, damage coastal areas, and increase conflict over scarce resources.[8] The desert regions of the Sahara and the Sahel in northern Africa and the drier regions in the south could be particularly hard hit. One Stanford University study found that by 2030 southern African maize production could fall 30 percent, and production of several other crops (millet, cow pea, wheat) could fall 10–15 percent.[9]

The emerging African countries, along with many other developing countries, will have to adapt to these changing circumstances.[10] In most countries, since agriculture is likely to be the hardest-hit sector, efforts

---

7 David Blair, "Rioters Attack Chinese after Zambian Poll," *The Daily Telegraph,* October 3, 2006, http://www.telegraph.co.uk/news/worldnews/1530464/Rioters-attack-Chinese-after-Zambian-poll.html.

8 See World Bank, *Development and Climate Change,* World Development Report 2010 (Washington, DC: World Bank, 2010).

9 David Lobell, et al., "Prioritizing Climate Change Adaptation Needs for Food Security in 2030," *Science* 319: 607–610.

10 See Edward Miguel, *Africa's Turn?* (Cambridge, MIT Press, 2009).

to increase agricultural productivity and to diversify production—both to other crops and to nonagricultural activities—are imperative. Among other things, this points to the need to develop drought-resistant crops, build better rural infrastructure (especially feeder roads and irrigation), and manage scarce water resources more effectively. It also suggests the need for appropriate pricing, including reducing subsides for (and shifting to taxes on) petroleum products and water-intensive crops, and perhaps creating incentives for private insurance markets. Countries must manage forest resources better since deforestation is a major contributor to CO_2 emissions. And they will need to adopt new green technologies in energy production (including second-generation biomass fuels), housing construction, and other areas that increase energy efficiency.

Many components of the appropriate response are sensible even in the absence of climate change, including increased agricultural productivity, more efficient use of energy, and better management of ecosystems. But these actions become even more urgent given the likely trends of the coming decades. The emerging countries themselves can have only a small direct impact on climate change, but their actions, and the support they receive from rich countries for their actions, will have a big impact on how their countries are affected. The countries that adopt sensible policies early on will be much better positioned to adapt to climate change and minimize the impacts on economic growth and poverty reduction in the future.

5. Building strong education and health systems.

Education and health are the building blocks of strong societies. There are few things more important for a country than to invest in its people. While the emerging countries have made important initial progress in education and health in recent years, they still have far to go. With respect to education, the increases in school enrollment and completion rates, especially for girls, are good first steps. Yet school quality suffers from outdated curricula, inadequate facilities, weak teacher training, insufficient local control, absenteeism, and poor pay. Students who complete school do not have the skills necessary even for the most basic jobs. While the focus in recent decades, appropriately, has been on primary education, the emerging countries must focus on rebuilding secondary and tertiary education. Some of Africa's great universities were gutted during the years of crisis, and they must be reinvigorated to build the skills of the economic and political leaders of the next generation.

Similarly, the improvements in health in recent years are a welcome beginning. There have been steady increases in immunization coverage rates and vigorous efforts to address specific diseases, especially HIV/

AIDS but also malaria, tuberculosis, river blindness, and polio. However, public health systems remain weak, underfunded, and overburdened. Robust efforts will be needed to improve access to health facilities and trained providers, improve the delivery of an integrated package of basic health services, and strengthen and sustain health systems more broadly, in order to sustain the progress in growth, development, and poverty reduction.

One of the greatest challenges will be the fight against HIV/AIDS. There has been much progress. More than 2 million people in Africa are now receiving life-saving antiretroviral treatment, and the number of AIDS deaths in Africa began to decline for the first time in 2005. There is much greater awareness and more effective education, prevention, care, and treatment programs. In some countries, the number of new infections is declining. In 10 of the 14 emerging countries for which data are available, the percentage of people living with HIV (the prevalence rate) has fallen, led by a sharp decline in Uganda and welcome initial declines in Rwanda, Tanzania, Botswana, and other countries (Figure 8.1).[11]

Nevertheless, as fewer people die from AIDS, the number of people living with the disease continues to grow. Education efforts have made some inroads, but ignorance remains widespread. Stigma against people with the virus remains a huge problem. And as welcome as the sharp rise in the number of people receiving treatment is, the current dynamics in treatment are creating unsustainable financial burdens, since each person will require treatment for decades to come.[12]

Ultimately, the HIV epidemic cannot be reversed without much more effective prevention programs to reduce the rate of new infections. Unfortunately, neither donor programs nor most country efforts focus enough attention on prevention. Going forward, the emerging countries and others must expand HIV education and behavior change programs, prevent mother-to-child transmission, and promote proven prevention strategies such as male circumcision, abstinence and faithfulness programs, condom use, and treatment of other sexually transmitted infections.

At the same time, while HIV/AIDS programs require significant resources, these efforts must be balanced against the need to strengthen health systems more broadly and to strengthen programs to combat other diseases, some of which—such as malaria—kill more people than HIV/AIDS. Getting the balance right for prevention, care, and treatment, and

---

11 All data in this section are drawn from UNAIDS/WHO, *2008 Report on the Global AIDS Epidemic* (Geneva: UNAIDS, 2008).

12 For an analysis of this issue, see Mead Over, "Prevention Failure: The Ballooning Entitlement Burden of U.S. Global AIDS Treatment Spending and What to Do About It," CGD Working Paper no. 144, May 2008, http://www.cgdev.org/content/publications/detail/15973.

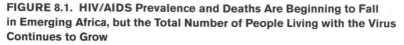

FIGURE 8.1. HIV/AIDS Prevalence and Deaths Are Beginning to Fall in Emerging Africa, but the Total Number of People Living with the Virus Continues to Grow

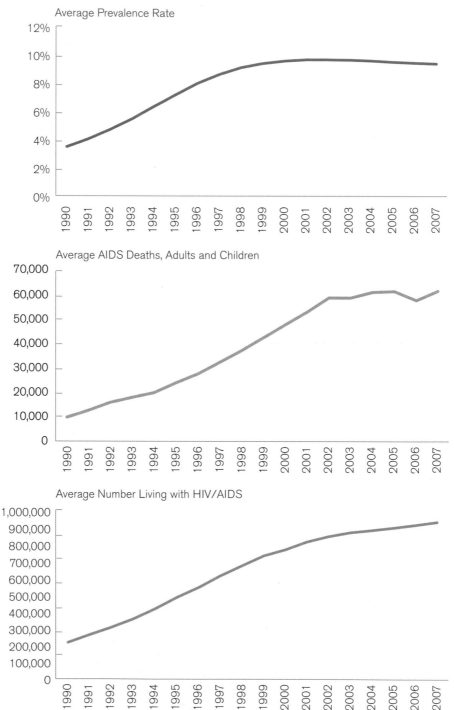

Source: UNAIDS, *2008 Report on the Global AIDS Epidemic* (Geneva: UNAIDS, 2008), available at http://www.unaids.org/en/KnowledgeCentre/HIVData/GlobalReport/2008/2008_Global_report.asp.

between HIV/AIDS programs and other urgent health priorities, will present major challenges for the emerging countries and others across Africa in years to come.

Unleashing the Power of Girls and Women

Girls and women are Africa's most underutilized asset. Meeting the challenges described above and sustaining the renaissance in emerging Africa will hinge on each country's ability to fully develop and take advantage of the skills and attributes of women and girls.[13] The returns on investing in girls and women are huge. When Lawrence Summers was chief economist of the World Bank, he argued that "investment in the education of girls may well be the highest-return investment available in the developing world."[14] Investing in girls' education increases the skill base, reduces fertility and population growth rates, reduces maternal and child mortality, and improves the educational and health opportunities for the next generation. Core public services depend on a strong cadre of teachers, health workers, engineers, lawyers, agricultural extension workers, and law enforcement officials, and capacity shortages in most of the emerging countries in these areas will not be fully met without adequately training women and girls in these fields. And continuing to strengthen governance will require women and girls to participate fully as citizens and become leaders in government, civil society, and business.

The emerging countries have made significant progress increasing the role of and opportunities for women and girls in recent years. Girls' enrollment rates have increased, health indicators have improved, more women are participating in the workforce, and there are a growing number of women legislators, ministers, and other political leaders. Liberia became the first African country to elect a woman as head of state in 2005 with the election of Ellen Johnson Sirleaf, putting it ahead of the United States, Japan, and much of Europe on that score.

Yet in too many countries women are restricted from owning property, shut out from financing opportunities, kept out of school, under-represented in senior government and political positions, passed over for job and management opportunities, and vulnerable to violence and abuse in

---

13 For an excellent analysis of these issues and opportunities, see Ruth Levine et al., *Girls Count: A Global Investment and Action Agenda* (Washington, DC: Center for Global Development, 2008). A terrific book on the topic is Nicholas Kristof and Sheryl WuDunn, *Half the Sky: Turning Oppression into Opportunity for Women Worldwide* (New York: Alfred A. Knopf, 2009).

14 Lawrence H. Summers, "Investing in All the People," World Bank Policy Research Working Paper WPS 905, May 1992, 1.

their own homes. Much more can and should be done to build legal environments that treat women and girls fairly, deliver social services more equitably, put more girls in school, and fight violence and discrimination against women and girls. Countries must ensure that public works and employment programs target women and girls, and remove the barriers that prevent women from ascending to private sector and government leadership positions.[15] If the emerging countries are to accelerate economic growth and build vibrant democracies in the future, they must unleash the intellectual, economic, and political power of women.

The Role of the International Community

As Africa's emerging countries continue to remain peaceful and make quiet progress in growth and development, it will be tempting for the rest of the world to ignore them and concentrate their energies on more problematic states. But this would be a terrible mistake. The emerging countries are becoming safer, more stable, and more responsible. They are moving along a path that is not only in their own best interests, but in the best interests of their neighbors and of the rest of the world. But while they have made significant progress, they remain fragile and their continued progress is far from assured. Even if they make the right decisions at home, regional or global forces could throw them off track. So while the actions of the emerging countries are the key to continuing their own progress, the international community has an important supporting role to play, especially in aid and trade.

Aid

As we have stressed, aid is not the most critical factor in determining the success or failure of the emerging countries. But it has provided important support for many of these countries in their turnaround, notably Burkina Faso, Ghana, Mali, Mozambique, Tanzania, Uganda, and Zambia, as it did earlier in Botswana and Mauritius, which for many years were two of the largest aid recipients in Africa. Aid's record in these countries is much more positive than the harshest critics claim. Botswana, Mauritius, Namibia, and South Africa have developed to the point that large amounts of aid are no longer so important (except for funding to fight

---

15 Ibid., 4–5.

HIV/AIDS and other diseases). For those with lower incomes and more fragile economies, aid still has an important role to play. But it has to be provided well and differently in the emerging countries. Taking the following three steps will help.

1. **Donors must ensure that the emerging countries—not the donors—have the lead in establishing priorities and designing and implementing programs.**

   The emerging countries deserve this respect; they have shown that they are capable of establishing priorities and making decisions that support growth and development. A deeper consultative process with governments, business leaders, and civil society requires time, patience, and a willingness to reorient priorities to match those of the recipients (such as more funding for infrastructure and agriculture). But it is central to building capacity, gaining legitimacy, and forging commitment from the range of actors necessary to ensure success.

2. **Donors should make larger and longer-term commitments to the emerging countries than they do to other countries.**

   More money is not everything, but it certainly helps. Across the emerging countries there are major funding shortfalls for critical public investments, and these countries have begun to show they can use funding well. More money better spent will not guarantee success, but it will certainly raise the odds, especially if the commitments are made for longer periods of time, such as for five years, to lend the certainty of sustained funding.

3. **Each party involved needs to be held more accountable for achieving results.**

   Aid programs should have clear, reasonable, and measurable goals, and progress against those goals should be assessed publicly on a regular basis. Organizations such as the United States' Millennium Challenge Corporation and the Global Fund to Fight AIDS, Tuberculosis and Malaria are on the forefront of focusing on results, and other donors are beginning to take steps in this direction.

Trade

In addition to aid, trade is clearly one of the most powerful instruments to sustain growth and provide a path out of poverty. But while rich countries have preached the benefits of free trade to poor countries for 30 years, they have erected barriers against products from poor countries that make this challenge all the more difficult.

There are two particularly egregious problems. The first is subsidies and protection on agricultural products in Japan, Europe, and the United States. Through various combinations of high tariffs, quotas, and subsidies, the rich countries create a distinctly unlevel playing field tilted against producers in poor countries. This protection extends to a wide range of products: cotton, dairy products, maize, peanuts, soybeans, sugar, rice, and wheat, among others. The second problem is that rich countries apply higher tariffs on finished goods produced from raw materials than they do on the raw materials themselves. For example, the United States charges no duty on raw cocoa beans, but imposes duties as high as 52 cents per kilogram on imported chocolate.[16] The European Union and Japan follow similar practices. These polices undermine the incentives for low-income countries to do exactly what they need to do—diversify into downstream production and sell the finished products abroad. The rich world makes it harder for poor countries to do what they need to do to succeed.

The best solution would be to eliminate these barriers and subsidies and level the playing field. Unfortunately, the failure of the Doha Round of trade talks and the fact that rich countries have actually increased these barriers in recent years make such an outcome unlikely any time soon. But there is scope to do more through preferential agreements, such as the United State's African Growth and Opportunity Act (AGOA), and the EU's Everything But Arms (EBA) Initiative, and to aim them more specifically at countries like the emerging countries with records of good governance. Rich countries can simplify the documentation and approval processes, simplify rules of origin, and consider expanding the range of products covered by these trade arrangements. They also can expand programs that provide technical support and business and market advice to build the capacity of firms trying to take advantage of these programs. And they can expand export financing and investment insurance programs to support exporting firms.

Beyond aid, trade, and similar instruments, world leaders can provide powerful support by vocally standing with the emerging countries. We should not underestimate the importance to governments, business leaders, local press, civil society leaders, and citizens of seeing and hearing strong signs of support from world leaders. What can sometimes seem a small gesture can take on big meaning in these countries. Visits from heads of state or senior ministers to the emerging countries, visits by the

---

16 FAO, "Agricultural Commodities: Profiles and Relevant WTO Negotiating Issues," background document for the Consultation on Agricultural Commodity Price Problems, March 25–26, 2002, http://www.fao.org/DOCREP/006/Y4343E/Y4343E00.HTM.

leaders of the emerging countries to major capitals, invitations to summits and other high-profile meetings, reference to the emerging countries in speeches and statements by world leaders, and other similar actions are more than empty gestures—they are signs of respect. Announcements such as the selection of countries by the Millennium Challenge Corporation can have important meaning beyond the programs that follow.

Like people all around the world, the citizens and leaders of the emerging countries want credibility and respect for their efforts and progress, and they deserve it. They are tired of being seen as part of a so-called failed continent and eagerly welcome recognition of their turnaround. Gaining such respect helps them to further advance the agenda of strengthening economic policy and deepening democracy. It is not easy to push continually for economic and political reform, since there are powerful groups within each of the emerging countries that are resisting more open and broad-based economic and political systems. Having world leaders stand with them helps them to gain credibility, push back on resistance, and strengthen the foundation for continued progress.

Finally, it is time for journalists, analysts, and commentators to move beyond the storyline that all of sub-Saharan Africa is a continent that has failed to make progress, mired in conflict, corruption, and hopelessness. Of course they should point out problems where they exist and push for change, but it is time to move away from the continent-wide generalizations of failure. That story is at least 15 years out of date. It does a tremendous disservice to the leaders and citizens of the emerging countries that have taken the risks and made the tough choices to begin to turn around their countries. They deserve much better than to continue to be painted with the same brush as those countries that have not done so.

✳ ✳ ✳

It is possible that the renaissance in the emerging countries could stall. Perhaps we may look back at the 1995–2010 period as a welcome but brief interlude between the end of the Cold War and the beginning of the global financial crisis in which some African countries were able to make short-lived progress that was later reversed. To be sure, question marks remain. But I don't think that will be the case.

The single most important country that will shape the future of the region is, beyond question, South Africa. It has the largest and most sophisticated economy on the continent, the engine that powers the entire southern region. Just as its emergence from apartheid led the way to greater freedom and opportunity around the region in the early 1990s, its continued political and economic progress is crucial to leading the way in the future. Concerns about South Africa's future were heightened during the messy presidential transition from Thabo Mbeki to Kgalema Motlanthe to Jacob Zuma in 2008 and 2009. Early signs do not indicate a significant shift in economic policy, but if South Africa does take a turn for the worse, all bets are off.

Ghana will also be critical. Oil production, which is to begin in late 2010, is expected to earn the country billions each year. The question is whether the oil windfall will be invested wisely and help propel Ghana to middle-income status, or whether it will be a poison pill. Or to put it another way, will Ghana follow Botswana or Nigeria? Botswana was able to manage its diamond windfall successfully because it had put into place basic institutions of democracy and good governance before the boom; it was accountable and transparent with the revenues; it maintained macroeconomic stability; and it reinvested the money in roads, power, schools, and clinics that provided the basis for sustained growth. In Nigeria, by contrast, oil fueled corruption and violence, generated intense instability, and undermined the incentives for a range of economic activities, most importantly agricultural production. Botswana is far better off for having found diamonds; Nigeria is far worse off for having found oil. Time will tell which path Ghana chooses.

Beyond the emerging countries themselves, much depends on the other countries in SSA that have yet to turn the corner. The emerging countries provide encouraging examples that better governance, sustained growth, and poverty reduction are possible. Several countries have recently taken the first steps along the path of the emerging countries, including Kenya, Liberia, and Sierra Leone. One hopes that others in SSA will take similar steps and join the group in the years to come. By far the most important is Nigeria. Nigeria has come far since the death of Sani Abacha in 1998, but its progress has been uneven, and its transition to democracy has fallen well short of expectations. For the people of Nigeria and West Africa more broadly, much hangs in the balance with Nigeria's future.

All of Africa's emerging countries will face economic and political challenges in the years ahead, and it is easy to be pessimistic. But there are good reasons to be optimistic that they can continue their progress—halting and uneven, but nonetheless progress—and that their examples can be extended to other countries in the region. It will not be easy, and it surely will not just happen automatically. It will require hard work, difficult choices, and strong efforts by their citizens, with support from their partners abroad. But that's exactly what they have done for the last 15 years.

Things have changed in Africa's emerging countries. There is a genuine sense of hope for the future. The changes are not just better numbers, and they are not just a temporary blip on the screen. They are deeper, and more fundamental, and are translating into better lives for people across the continent. They have been quietly under way for 15 years, long enough to give them some credibility, and some roots. These countries must now prove whether their progress can be sustained. They deserve credit and recognition for what they have accomplished. And they deserve patience and support as they move forward, because success cannot be achieved overnight.

The emerging countries have shown that nations that were once considered failures and that were stuck in conflict and stagnation can turn around and begin the arduous climb out of poverty. That is good news indeed. It provides hope for some of the toughest places in the world to further combat poverty, increase prosperity, secure peace, and widen the global circle of development.

INDEX

Page numbers in *italic* refer to illustrations or tables.

arap Moi, Daniel, 31, 60–61, 132
Authoritarian governments
    decline of, 51–54
    economic performance and, 18, 50–52
    foreign aid to, 99
    post-Colonial establishment of, 49–54
    risk of return of, 60, 145
    support from developed countries for, during
      Cold War, 1, 53
Awuah, Patrick, 125–26
Ayittey, George, 126–27

B
Ba, Amadou, 129–30
Babangida, Ibrahim, 49
Banda, Rupiah, 61
Banking. *See* Financial services
Banks, Arthur, 64
Barkan, Joel, 144
Bates, Robert, 50–51, 52, 74
Beer, Ron, 133–34
Benin
    economic performance of, 31
    political environment in, 54
    See also Threshold countries
Binagwaho, Agnes, 128–29
Bono, 127
Botswana, 76
    business environment of, 85
    economic growth of, 33–34, 158
    foreign aid to, 99
    foreign exchange reserves of, 81
    life expectancy in, 39
    political environment in, 50, 62
    South Africa and, 23–24
    See also Emerging countries
Bottom Billion, The (Collier), 22, 100
Bratton, Michael, 52
Burkina Faso
    business environment of, 85
    Song-Taaba Yalgré, 109–10
    See also Emerging countries
Burundi, 69
Business environment
    benefits of technology for, 110–11, 114–19
    in emerging countries, 14, 35–37, *87*
    evolution in sub-Saharan Africa, 1, 74, 75, 84–87
    Ghana's, 72
    investment patterns, 35–37, 87
    Liberia's, 3

Mozambique's, 10
new generation of leaders and entrepreneurs,
    129, 135–36
obstacle to economic growth, 76
productivity, 37, *38*
recent evolution in sub-Saharan Africa, 1
start-up costs, 84–85, *85*
transparency in natural resources contracting,
    144–45

C
Cape Verde
    economic performance of, 10, 33
    educational system of, 10
    income patterns in, 10
    infant mortality in, 10
    political environment in, 10, 54, 62
    poverty patterns and trends in, 10
    remittances to, 118
    tourism industry of, 39
    trade patterns, 10
    See also Emerging countries
Cell phones. *See* Mobile phone technology
Chiluba, Frederick, 53
China, 25, 37, 147–49
Civil liberties
    economic growth and, 18
    evolution in sub-Saharan Africa, 53–54
    indicators of democratic systems, 68
    trends in emerging countries, 14, 58–59, 62, 73
Civil society
    benefits of communication technology, 121
    new generation of leaders in Africa, 125–39
    trends in sub-Saharan Africa, 59–62, 88
Civil war
    Liberia's, 1–2
    Mozambique's, 27
Climate change, 24, 149–50
Clinton Foundation, 104
Coffee, 43
Cold War, 1, 17, 23, 27, 47, 53, 95
Collier, Paul, 21–22, 23, 88, 100
Communications technology
    access to finance improved by, 117–19
    African market for, 111–12
    economic benefits of, 20, 110–11, 114–17
    employment in, 116–17
    future prospects of, 112–14, 119, 122–23
    governance applications, 121–22
    health care applications, 119–20

to improve trade and customs procedures, 122
literacy issues and, 116
malicious use of, 121
mobile phones, 20, 110–15, 118–19
political accountability and transparency
    improved by, 120–21
productivity gains from, 114
significance of, in Africa, 114
trends, 20, 110, 111–12, *113*
Comoros, 54, 55
Computer technology, 109–10. *See also* Technology
Congo, Democratic Republic of, 11, 69
Congo, Republic of, 55
Corruption, 66, 74, 120–21, 137–38
Côte d'Ivoire, 69
Cuba, 48

D

Debt
    debt-to-export ratios, 91–92, 93, 96, *97*
    economic shocks of 1970s and 1980s, 51–52,
        91–92, 97
    future prospects, 96–98
    outcomes of 1980s debt crisis, 92–94
    reasons for resurgence of emerging countries, 5
    recent African history, 10, 18–19, 96, *97*
    resolution of 1980s debt crisis, 95–96
Democratic processes
    as basis for success of emerging countries, 5, 16
    in Botswana, 50
    in Cape Verde, 10, 62
    competitiveness, 56, *56*
    in Democratic Republic of Congo, 69
    economic growth and, 18, 66, 143
    in Ethiopia, 62, 145
    executive branch elections, 56
    future challenges and opportunities, 60, 142–44,
        145
    in The Gambia, 50, 60
    in Ghana, 73, 145
    governance quality and, 64, 66
    historical evolution in sub-Saharan Africa, 50,
        54–57, 145
    indicators of, 68–69
    institutional capacity for, 57
    legislative branch elections, 56
    in Mali, 10, 35
    in Mauritius, 50
    in Mozambique, 27, 62
    in Namibia, 47, 48–49

in Nigeria, 69
peaceful transfers of power in sub-Saharan
    Africa, 57, *58*
poverty and, 55
recent evolution of sub-Saharan Africa, 1, 16, 17,
    60–62
in Rwanda, 62, 145
in Tanzania, 10, 69
in threshold countries, *65*
trends in Africa, 3, 4, 9, 14, 16
trends in emerging countries, 62, *63, 65,* 69, 141
in Uganda, 62, 145
Developed countries
    Africa's trading partners, 37–39
    economic growth of, 31
    emerging countries' relationships with donor
        community from, 19
    expressions of support for emerging nations
        from leaders of, 156–57
    support for African dictators given by, in Cold
        War era, 1, 53
    trade barriers in, 106, 155–56
Diamond, Larry, 59–60
Djibouti, 69
Djiguiba, Ansema, 59
Djiguiba, Sulamo, 59
Doe, Samuel, 49

E

Economic Growth in Africa, 17, 76
Economic performance
    of agricultural sector, 35, 36, 74, 82–84
    antigrowth syndromes and, 17–18, 76, 78
    under authoritarian governments of sub-Saha-
        ran Africa, 18, 50–52
    basis for success of emerging countrics, 17,
        22–23, 43–44
    benefits of technology for, 20, 109–11, 114–19
    Botswana's, 33–34
    Cape Verde's, 10, 33
    characteristics of emerging countries, 30–31
    Chinese investment in sub-Saharan Africa,
        147–49
    commodity price patterns and, 43–44
    debt crisis of 1980s, 91–92
    development traps affecting, 21–22
    effects of neighboring countries' performance,
        23–24
    in emerging countries, 13, 14, *32,* 32–35, 141
    future challenges and opportunities, 24–25,
        87–89, 145–47

emergence of women in leadership positions, 131–32
factors contributing to successes of emerging countries, 5, 20
future challenges and opportunities, 24
in The Gambia, 60, 61
in Ghana, 9, 61
history of authoritarian rule in sub-Saharan Africa, 1, 49–51
in Kenya, 60–61
leadership capacity, 5, 20, 66, 88, 125–26
in Liberia, 2
in Mali, 10, 35
in Mozambique, 10, 27
in Namibia, 47–49
new generation of leaders in Africa, 125–39
recent evolution in sub-Saharan Africa, 1
term limits, 57
in threshold countries, 62
transfers of power in sub-Saharan Africa, 57, *58*
trends in emerging countries, 4, 14
violent conflict in, 64, 65
young voters, 137
in Zambia, 61
See also Accountability and transparency; Democratic processes; Governance; Policy development, generally
Populations patterns and trends
in emerging countries, 12, 13, 14, 41, *41*
fertility rates, 41
in Ghana, 2
Posner, Daniel, 57
Poverty
in Cape Verde, 10
data sources, *9n*
development traps concept, 21–22
in emerging countries, 5, 14, 34, 141
foreign aid programs to reduce, 101–2
in Ghana, 2, *72*
in Mali, 10, 35
in Mozambique, 10, 28
prospects for democratization and, 55
in sub-Saharan Africa, 76
Press, freedom of, 59, 88
Privatization
economic recovery in sub-Saharan Africa, 78
in Mozambique, 27–28
Productivity, 37, *38*
in agricultural sector, 146
benefits of technology, 114
Property registration, 86

Q
Quadir, Iqbal, 114
Quartey, Doris, 73

R
Rawlings, Jerry, 55, 72
Remittances into Africa, 118
Rhodesia, 27
Rutagumirwa, Laban, 110
Rwanda
business environment in, 86
foreign aid to, 99
foreign exchange reserves of, 81
health care in, 40–41, 128–29
political environment in, 62, 145
tourism industry, 39, 147
See also Emerging countries

S
Sachs, Jeffrey, 21–22
São Tomé and Principe, 54, 81. *See also* Emerging nations
Sata, Michael, 61, 148–49
Satellite communications, 112
Sawadogo, Awa, 110
Sayeh, Antoinette, 132
Senegal
economic performance of, 31, 116
political environment in, 55
See also Threshold countries
Shyan, Lee Yi, *see* Lee Yi Shyan
Sierra Leone
business environment in, 85
economic growth of, 31
political environment in, 55, 120
See also Threshold countries
Silva Herzog, Jesús, 91
Singapore, 37
Sirleaf, Ellen Johnson, 55, 128, 131, 153
Soludo, Chukwuma, 88
Somalia, 11
Soros Economic Development, 104
South Africa
apartheid era, 27
business environment in, 85
economic growth of, 23
future challenges and opportunities for, 158
MobileMoney, 119
Namibia and, 48
political environment in, 54
role in regional development, 23–24

PRAISE FOR *EMERGING AFRICA*

"In this original and rigorous analysis of Africa's emerging turnaround, Steve Radelet demolishes a host of outdated assumptions about the continent's diffuse economic and political failures. With a wealth of data and the cool but sympathetic lens of a development economist deeply experienced in the region, Radelet shows how 17 African countries are emerging out of poverty and stagnation—and how others could follow—through democracy, improved governance, more sensible economic policies, new communication technologies, and a new generation of more able and committed leaders. If you read one book on where Africa is headed, make it this one."

— **Larry Diamond,** *Director, Center on Democracy, Development, and the Rule of Law, Stanford University*

"*Emerging Africa* explains how domestic developments and international support led to sub-Saharan Africa's growth turnaround since the mid-1990s. Steve Radelet's comprehensive analysis provides further grounds for optimism that improved macroeconomic management in a significant number of countries is producing tangible results, including resilience to recent shocks. It makes an important contribution to mounting evidence of sustainable economic improvements across the continent, while being realistic about the effort needed to tackle remaining challenges."

— **Antoinette Monsio Sayeh,** *former Minister of Finance for Liberia and Director, African Department, International Monetary Fund*

"In this important study, Steve Radelet teaches us to look at Africa afresh. In much of the continent, there is economic growth rather than decline, political order rather than violence, and political competition rather than authoritarianism. Much of Africa is succeeding, economically and politically. Attend to this book!"

— **Robert H. Bates,** *Eaton Professor of the Science of Government, Harvard University*

"*Emerging Africa* will fundamentally change the way that Westerners think about sub-Saharan Africa—no longer as a basket case, but as a region in which good policies have paved the way to economic progress and democratic government. It is a good antidote to the peddlers of global pessimism."

— **Francis Fukuyama,** *Stanford University*

"Steve Radelet has given us good news out of Africa—not wishful thinking, but solid evidence that nearly half of the countries of sub-Saharan Africa have experienced significant and sustained economic growth over the past decade and a half. This well-written, balanced, and insightful account of economic performance in the region gives hope that African countries can overcome their challenges and break out of poverty traps with good policies, effective institutions, and good luck. The book is a major contribution to the literature on development in the region and should be read by all those who have an interest in Africa or in development."

— **Carol Lancaster,** *Dean, Edmund A. Walsh School of Foreign Service, Georgetown University*

"A number of recent studies have described how Africa has grown relatively rapidly over the past 15 years. Steve Radelet's book tells us why and shows how this growth may be sustained and shared more broadly. This lucid, rigorous, and compelling book is a fitting tribute to a dynamic continent."

— **Shanta Devarajan,** *Chief Economist for the Africa region, World Bank*

"Over the past 15 years, Mozambique has emerged as one of the fastest growing economies in the world; Ghana has slashed its poverty rate; Mali has doubled school enrollment; Tanzania has cut infant mortality by a quarter. In this brilliantly lucid book, Steve Radelet explains the economic, political, and technological forces behind the remarkable progress in 17 African countries."

— **Sebastian Mallaby,** *Paul A. Volcker Senior Fellow for International Economics, Council on Foreign Relations*

"Success is under way in Africa. In this invaluable book, we begin to understand where, how, and why. Radelet shows that in at least 17 non-oil economies, a process of favorable economic and political transformation has been under way since the mid-1990s. His analysis is balanced, convincing, and timely—and the trends will not be easily reversed. This narrative of accomplishment and hope is indispensable for an informed view of what is happening in Africa and what lies ahead."

— **Stephen A. O'Connell,** *Eugene M. Lang Research Professor of Economics, Swarthmore College*

"This engaging and well-researched gem of a book should be required reading for students, policymakers, and journalists. Steve Radelet convincingly makes two underappreciated arguments: First, to understand 'Africa' and the changes that have occurred since the mid-1990s, its strongest performers must be disaggregated from the weak because they have achieved a measure of economic growth and poverty reduction thought unlikely a decade ago. Second, the key to economic progress has been the progress toward democratic governance. Supported by a wealth of time-series data, Radelet demonstrates that, for Africa, the Chinese model does not apply."

— **Joel D. Barkan,** *Senior Associate, Center for Strategic and International Studies*